TWENTIETH CENTURY VIEWS

The aim of this series is to present the best in
contemporary critical opinion on major authors,
providing a twentieth century perspective on
their changing status in an era of profound
revaluation.

Maynard Mack, *Series Editor*
Yale University

POE

POE

A COLLECTION OF CRITICAL ESSAYS

Edited by

Robert Regan

Prentice-Hall, Inc. A SPECTRUM BOOK *Englewood Cliffs, N. J.*

Contents

Introduction

by Robert Regan

To say that Edgar Poe has been the least understood of America's major writers would invite a fruitless debate, but surely no one will deny that he has been the most *mis*understood. What other figure in our literature has been so persistently, so pertinaciously, so perversely misrepresented by biographers and critics alike? Until the appearance in 1880 of J. H. Ingram's adulatory *Edgar Allan Poe: His Life, Letters, and Opinions,* the Rev. R. W. Griswold's memoir, an account of Poe's life full of calumnies supported by lies and forgeries, remained virtually the only source of information available to the public. It is principally to Griswold's jealousy and malice that we may trace the image of Poe as the evil genius of American letters. Yet Griswold had help enough in establishing the image of the *poète maudit* who would become, and remain, the villainous hero of the Poe myth: Poe himself had contributed to the myth by misrepresenting the outlines of his biography, and in his ten years as a critic and literary combatant he had made scores of enemies who were ready to do their share in blackening his name. Only four years after Poe's death the legend had reached Scotland and the Rev. George Gilfillan, who wrote that

> Poets, as a tribe, have been rather a worthless, wicked set of people; and certainly Edgar A. Poe, instead of being an exception, was probably *the* most worthless and wicked of all his fraternity. . . . He was no more a gentleman than he was a saint. His heart was as rotten as his conduct was infamous. . . . He had absolutely no virtue or good quality, unless you call remorse a virtue, and despair a grace. . . . He was, in short, a combination in almost equal proportions, of the fiend, the brute, and the genius.

A few of Gilfillan's contemporaries were even less generous: some went so far as to deny that the fiendish brute had also earned the name of genius. It was the opinion of Henry James that "an enthusiasm for Poe is the mark of a decidedly primitive stage of reflection. It seems to us," he continued, "that to take him with more than a certain degree of seriousness is to lack seriousness one's self."

Not all that Ingram could say in Poe's behalf could dispel the climate of opinion which the libels of Griswold and his tribe had created. If Poe's admirers had confidence that time and truth would join forces to restore his reputation, they were doomed to disappointment. Not even Arthur H. Quinn's definitive and essentially favorable *Edgar Allan Poe: A Critical Biography*, which appeared in 1941, has silenced the voice of slander. Nor have the high estimates of the poetry and the tales which have come from critics of the caliber of Baudelaire, Mallarmé, Bernard Shaw, Paul Valéry, and William Carlos Williams succeeded in discrediting Henry James's dismissal of Poe. Indeed, the spirit of James's judgment seems to inform much recent criticism. Probably the best known twentieth century estimates of Poe's work have come from T. S. Eliot, who charged him with "slipshod writing," and Yvor Winters, who damned him for "obscurantism."

It is astonishing that such opinions persist in a period when a majority of the critics, scholars, and writers who have troubled themselves to read extensively in Poe's works have agreed that his accomplishments were major. They have agreed, furthermore, that his accomplishments were major in all three areas of his endeavor, in fiction, in poetry, and in criticism. In this respect his distinction is singular, perhaps even unique among American writers of his century.

Poe's criticism merits our attention first of all because his judgments were remarkably often both original and right. Many of his reviews, let me acknowledge at the outset, do his reputation no service. Too often he petulantly derided good works by men he envied; sometimes he even accused a rival of "plagiarism"—by which he meant no more than that the offender's works showed the influence of some other writer—when in fact he had himself drawn heavily upon the works of the rival he condemned; and he was not above puffing inferior works on occasion, if by doing so he could secure favor, employment, and support from the leaders of one or another of the warring literary factions of his day. Most of his judgments, nevertheless, were considered and independent and they are noteworthy as much for their precociousness as for their validity. Consider the case of his famous comments on Hawthorne. In May of 1842, before any other critic of enduring reputation had recognized the merits of the newly published *Twice Told Tales,* Poe ended a long review in *Graham's Magazine* with these words: "The style is purity itself. Force abounds. High imagination gleams from every page. Mr. Hawthorne is a man of the truest genius. We only regret that the limits of our Magazine will not permit us to pay him that full tribute of commendation, which, under other circumstances, we should be so eager to pay."

Poe's gift for recognizing merit in the books he reviewed was remarkable; but even more remarkable, and even rarer, was his capacity to see the criticism of his time as if from a vantage point outside it. Again and again he demonstrated that he grasped as few of his contemporaries could what was enduring and what was merely ephemeral in the critical practice of the 1830s and 1840s. One example will suggest the nature of his unusual ability. In the middle of the twentieth century, a student of Shakespeare criticism has no difficulty detecting that the chief shortcoming of nineteenth century discussions of Shakespeare involves the treatment of character. In the last century emphasis on character as the controlling element in the plays tended to result in the error of discussing individual *dramatis personae* as if they had life outside the plays in which they appear. The tendency was to culminate (but not terminate) thirty years after Poe's death when Mary Cowden Clarke published *The Girlhood of Shakespeare's Heroines.* But in 1845, reviewing Hazlitt's *Characters of Shakespeare,* Poe was able—with justice, I believe— to boast that he was the first critic to identify the confusion in the Shakespeare commentary of the age:

> In all commentating upon Shakspeare, there has been a radical error, never yet mentioned. It is the error of attempting to expound his characters—to account for their actions—to reconcile his inconsistencies—not as if they were the coinage of a human brain, but as if they had been actual existences upon earth. We talk of Hamlet the man, instead of Hamlet the *dramatis persona*—of Hamlet that God, in place of Hamlet that Shakspeare created. If Hamlet had really lived, and if the tragedy were an accurate record of his deeds, from this record (with some trouble) we might, it is true, reconcile his inconsistencies and settle to our satisfaction his true character. But the

task becomes the purest absurdity when we deal only with a phantom.
. . . It seems to us little less than a miracle, that this obvious point
should have been overlooked.

The same review contains, by the way, a notable passage of uncommon common sense on the question of Hamlet's madness, another thorny problem in which many of Poe's contemporaries had entangled themselves.

On the broader question of what the limitations and the focus of aesthetic judgment ought to be, Poe was again at odds with his age—and in harmony with ours. The "Exordium" he prefaced to the review columns of *Graham's Magazine* in January 1842 states a critical precept which in the twentieth century would take priority over all others: "Following the highest authority, we would wish, in a word, to limit literary criticism to comment upon *Art*." This precept, which Poe restated again and again in reviews and articles, suffices to align him with that approach to literary judgment which the twentieth century, in a self-congratulatory mood, chose to call its *New* Criticism.

The accomplished writer who is also an accomplished critic is vulnerable to the accusation—more often than not an invidious accusation—that he has constructed an *ad hoc* critical system in justification of his practice as a creative artist. Poe, in company with such diverse figures as Wordsworth and Eliot, has been called to task on this account. In point of fact, the soundest argument which may be advanced for Poe's poems is that a substantial number of them succeed in embodying his theory of what poetry ought to be. His premise that "a poem deserves its title only inasmuch as it excites, by elevating the soul" and that "the value of the poem is in the ratio of this elevating excitement" is of help in understanding his accomplishments in poetry, and his failings as well. The excitement of one of Poe's best-known poems, "To Helen," mounts even as the poet's thoughts rise from the Helen he adores, first to her prototype in legend, Helen of Troy, and finally to her completely idealized archetype, "Psyche, from the regions which Are Holy-Land!" The music of that poem answers and accomplishes its emotional ascent. In another of his best-known poems, "The Raven," the form rather impedes the ascent. "The trouble with 'The Raven,'" W. H. Auden has observed, "is that the thematic interest and the prosodic interest, both of which are considerable, do not combine and are even often at odds." "The Raven" remains at best a curiosity because form and meaning do not cooperate to raise it to a peak of emotional intensity. Thus Poe's own poems seem to bear out his premise: their worth often stands in ratio to their "elevating excitement." If, however, we attempt to test the premise by applying it to other poets in other periods, we soon discover its limitations. If, for example, we attempt, rather perversely, to apply it to the verse of the Restoration and the eighteenth century, we will be tempted, half-seriously, to infer that certain of Rochester's poems would have displeased Poe because they do not elevate, however much they excite; certain of Dr. Johnson's because they do not excite, however much they may elevate. Yet what we are demanding when we stipulate that our definition of poetry must warrant our valuing "The Imperfect Enjoyment," "The Vanity of Human Wishes," *and* "To One in Paradise" is an inclusive aesthetic, a catholic theory of literature. If we grant that Poe's definition of poetry was exclusive, his conception of art parochial, we may nevertheless argue that his view of what a poem ought to be is an essential part of an inclusive and catholic aesthetic theory.

The case for the validity of Poe's theory and for the value of his accomplishment in poetry is stated enthusiastically and persuasively by the Irish novelist George Moore in his *Anthology of Pure Poetry* (1924). The introduction to that collection reports an after-dinner conversation Moore had with his friends Walter De La Mare and John Freeman. Although they advance no claim for its being the only true poetry, the three friends agree that what they call "pure poetry" deserves to be valued above any other kind. In their view the pure poem is one which recreates the objective world the poet hears and sees, abjuring subjective ideas such as *duty* and *liberty*. When the three decide to select a volume of poems which match their conception, De La Mare observes that they will "find many poems in Poe. . . . Our difficulty with Poe will be not to over-burden our pages with him." They agree that poems they select for their anthology ought not be longer than a hundred lines, and Moore recalls that this restriction was one of Poe's:

A hundred lines, I think, was the length that a poem should never exceed, according to Poe, and the reason he gives is that a poem should be read in one uninterrupted mood of increasing exaltation. He wrote little and I have never read that he wrote with ease, as Shelley did, but he wrote certainly out of an emotive imagination; his poems are absolutely free from thought, and that is why we have gathered so many in this tiny garden of our anthology. Another thing. He is one of the few modern poets who wrote with his eyes as well as his ears. . . .

In this passage Moore suggests what elements of Poe's accomplishments as poet validate his theory; in his selection of poems, Moore presents an even more convincing validation of Poe's theories. Yet one of the opinions Moore assigns to Freeman in the preliminary dialogue—an opinion in which Moore manifestly joins—warns us that any doctrine of pure poetry is apt to lead to an indefensibly narrow view of what is and what is not "real" poetry. Harping on the notion that propaganda, polemic, and dogma (or, as Moore would say, "thought") must be excluded from "objective" or "pure" poetry, Freeman delivers an opinion which can hardly fail to arouse our misgivings: "Milton does not abound in objective poetry, Pope still less, but we shall find several poems that come within our definition in the *Songs of Innocence,* none, I am afraid, in *Songs of Experience.*" True to that precept, Moore presents eight of Blake's poems in the anthology, all from *Songs of Innocence.* Poe's own conception of the boundaries of poetry was narrow, but not in the same sense: of that the range of his subject matter presents conclusive evidence. In what sense, then, was his view of the domain of poetry narrow?

In that extraordinary little book *What is Poetry,* John Hall Wheelock speaks of "the voice least often sounding in any poem, and in any poem the voice carrying farthest, best heard by the many, and the longest remembered. . . . When it speaks, it is as if it spoke *from* all of us *to* all of us." Such poetry, in which the unconscious touches the conscious for a fleeting moment, quite naturally calls Poe to Mr. Wheelock's mind, for this was the species of poetry Poe held to be the only real species. A passage from Poe's *Marginalia* (June 1849) contains a definition of *Art* in language which one might effortlessly paraphrase into terms like Mr. Wheelock's—or C. G. Jung's. "Were I called on to define, *very* briefly, the term 'Art,' " Poe wrote, "I should call it 'the reproduction of what the Senses perceive in Nature through the veil of the Soul.'" The "test of a poet's art and discipline," Mr. Wheelock contends, is his skill in producing a connective tissue of less exalted poetry which will hold the sublime passages together. It is at this point that the spirit of Poe might take issue and insist upon a narrower definition of poetry. The best poetry, Poe and other advocates of pure poetry would argue, is *all* poetry; the connective tissue must be cut away and discarded and the poetry which speaks "*from* all of us and *to* all of us" must be so wrought by the poet that it will stand alone and stand, however small a thing it may be, monumentally.

Poe's production of such small monuments of verse dates from the earliest years of his career—although we will do his reputation little real service if, with Lowell, we accept his substanceless story that he wrote "To Helen" when he was fourteen. (That nearly perfect poem was almost certainly completed after the 1829 publication of *Al Aaraaf, Tamerlane, and Minor Poems,* in which Poe would surely have included it had it been finished.) With each succeeding collection of his poems, he put the aesthetic precepts he was delivering in reviews and articles more and more rigorously into practice. The case of "The Valley of Unrest" is in many respects typical. In its successive revisions Poe intensified and unified the language of the poem, but he also reduced it from forty-six lines (1831) to twenty-seven lines (1845). And in such late poems as "Eldorado" and "For Annie," we see him endeavoring with undeniable success to achieve a unique effect in a lyric of some magnitude, and achieving that success in accordance with the precepts of his criticism by subordinating all the constituents of the poem— rhythm, imagery, rhyme, tone, meaning—to its governing totality. It would be well for all of us who admire Poe if we could forget his worst poems. ("The Raven" and "Ulalume," which seem to have been dictated by the Angel of the Odd, are my own nominees for bathetic eminence, but half a dozen other clinkers contest their claims.) Certainly, we shall have to enter a plea of guilty on his behalf to the charges of prosodic excess Aldous Huxley brings against him, although we may balk at the implied definitions of "vulgar" and "refined" writing by which Huxley prepares to assign Poe virtually *in toto* to the former class. Yet by the same token, we cannot permit either ourselves or Poe's detractors to disregard his best poems, or to forget that, as Floyd Stovall reminds us, "One does not arrive at the true worth of a literary artist by taking an average of his works."

The influence of Poe's poetry has been considerable, but the influence of his fiction has been even more widespread and far-reaching. Excessive claims have occasionally been made for Poe as a founder of science fiction, but enthusiasts of the detective story are in substantial agreement in hailing him as the founder of that genre. It was Poe, Jacques Barzun has observed, who first took the

> entrancing idea of detection and [made] it breed a distinctive literature by displaying it in an appropriate form. . . . "The Murders in the Rue Morgue," published in 1841, put an end to the episodic and casual use of detection. And when four years later Poe had written his three other detective tales, all the elements of the genre were at hand. What was to follow could only be elaboration, embellishment, and complication—most of it agreeable, some of it superior to the original in polish, but none of it transcending the first creation.

One might, I think, go somewhat further and say that Poe was more instrumental than any other writer in leading the whole genre of short fiction away from the episodic and casual.

The remarkable place Edgar Poe came to occupy in the history of French literature will be suggested by the chapter from Patrick F. Quinn's book on that subject reprinted in this collection. Outside France, one of the first European writers to respond to Poe was Doestoevsky, who wrote a laudatory article on several of the tales in 1861. The influence of "The Tell-Tale Heart" and the Dupin stories on *Crime and Punishment* has been convincingly demonstrated. The major American writers of the later nineteenth century were less inclined to speak well of Poe, but they were not free of his influence. In a letter to Howells, Mark Twain set down an accusation against Poe's style which is perhaps less damaging than he intended: "To me his prose is unreadable—like Jane Austen's. No, there is a difference. I could read his prose on salary, but not Jane's." Yet the treasure hunt in *Tom Sawyer* reveals that he recalled the details of "The Gold Bug" well enough to burlesque them. Furthermore, Walter Blair has pointed to Poe's "Four Beasts in One; or The Homocameleopard" as a possible source of The Royal Nonesuch in *Huckleberry Finn*. And I find more than coincidental similarities between Mark Twain's lighthearted story about a man who murders his conscience, "The Facts Concerning the Recent Carnival of Crime in Connecticut," and three of Poe's tales, "The Angel of the Odd," "The Imp of the Perverse," and "William Wilson." I have already quoted Henry James's best-known remark on Poe. Yet in such tales as "The Jolly Corner" and "The Turn of the Screw" we recognize a familiar forbidding ambience, the ambience of Poe's tales of horror. In James's tales, just as in "William Wilson" and "The Fall of the House of Usher," we confront ghostly figures who are the objectified, projected compulsions of the "real" characters. James's untrustworthy narrators may suggest another indebtedness to Poe. If so, it seems possible that James was guardedly repaying a debt when in the opening chapter of *The Golden Bowl* he allowed Prince Amerigo to recall that he had

> read, as a boy, a wonderful tale by Allan Poe, his prospective wife's countryman—which was a thing to show, by the way, what imagination Americans *could* have: the story of the shipwrecked Gordon Pym, who, drifting in a small boat further toward the North Pole—or was it the South?—than anyone had ever done, found at a given moment before him a thickness of white air that was like a dazzling curtain of light, concealing as darkness conceals, yet of the colour of milk or of snow.

W. H. Auden has called *The Narrative of Arthur Gordon Pym,* the work to which James's Prince Amerigo refers, "one of the finest adventure stories ever written, . . . an object lesson in the art." Surely *Gordon Pym* can be read as an adventure story, or, more precisely, as *two* adventure stories loosely concatenated, both of them attaining notable success; yet such a reading seems to claim at once too much and too little for the book which was Poe's only experiment with the novel. Better managed and more securely articulated tales of adventure abound in literature; but in *Gordon Pym* Poe was aiming at something more than a mere adventure story. He was attempting to survey a new world of the imagination and to cultivate it—a dark, inhospitable world. *Gordon Pym* proved a failure, but only in the sense that Sir Walter Raleigh's Roanoke Island was a failure. For in *Moby Dick* we have *Gordon Pym*'s Plymouth Plantation, and in scores of later works—works which continue to appear and enrich many literatures—the outgrowths of Poe's first ill-fated expedition into the appalling unknown flourish.

Whatever Poe's influence, whatever the import of his pioneering, our ultimate estimate of his importance must depend upon what he communicates to readers today, not upon what he may have conveyed to his literary heirs of previous generations. Because his tales are generally regarded as his most significant accomplishment, most of the essays in this collection focus upon that body of his writings. I feel impelled to add only one point to what those essays say about the tales.

Poe frequently expressed his distaste for allegory, possibly because he regarded any literary mode in which widely held ideas were expressed as deficient in originality. Here again, his practice echoes his precept: there is no Mr. Worldly Wiseman in Poe, no Mrs. Timorous; moral qualities are not given legs to totter on and nearly human voices in which to squeak out their names. Yet moral qualities for which we have no names in fact walk and speak in Poe's serious tales: there they acquire the motive force and the eloquence philosophy cannot give them; there they approach us and speak to us of what is true and of what is so mysterious as to confound our categories of truth and falsehood. Poe's tales move and speak symbolically.

Yet they do not speak in univocal symbols. Poe's best tales—so the essays in this collection will show—yield multiple meanings when we examine them closely. "The Fall of the House of Usher" is an exceptionally clear case in point. On the simplest literal level, that tale allows us to shiver as we hear the Lady Madeline ascending from the tomb of her premature burial toward the room where her transfixed brother awaits her inevitable coming. On that level the tale operates with perfect self-consistency, offering the very young reader the primitive pleasures of terror. The more perceptive reader will become aware in his second reading of "Usher" that Roderick suffers from an abnormal and utterly debilitating obsession; that this madman has by degrees drawn the initially sane narrator into a *folie à deux;* that while Madeline's body lies quiet in the tomb, the two friends share a series of hallucinations which culminate in their believing that they see the living corpse of Madeline in a dark and wind-swept hallway of the House of Usher.

We may say that this is what "really happens" in the story and we may support our conviction by observing that the tale is no less self-consistent when we read it as a record of mania than when we read it as a tale of simple horror. But we must add that it is also no *more* self-consistent: the two "literal" interpretations co-exist; they impinge upon one another only when our analysis presses them. And if these two literal readings are equally defensible—a situation which we can account for only by reference to Poe's great plotting skill—there remain other levels of meaning, other readings which we cannot ignore. Much recommends Richard Wilbur's contention that the tale dramatizes the *hypnagogic* state, a condition of semi-consciousness between sleep and waking in which, so Poe believed, the mind is singularly receptive to "glimpses of the spirit's outer world." In Mr. Wilbur's explication, "The House of Usher *is*, in allegorical fact, the physical body of Roderick Usher, and its dim interior *is*, in fact, Roderick Usher's visionary mind." Yet I also find much which compels assent to Maurice Beebe's view that Roderick is "a prototype of the artist-as-God" and the story a symbolic statement of the cosmological views Poe later set down in *Eureka*. Each of these readings attempts to illuminate a level of meaning which we may regard as conscious on Poe's part, but J.-P. Weber's analysis alerts us to a pattern of Oedipal significance in the tale which must have been unconscious, but which is not therefore the less convincing or the less revealing. Not one of these five levels of meaning fails to make its own case on the basis of self-consistency within the tale and of consistency with patterns discernible in Poe's other works. Yet the readings do not argue against each other; rather they complement each other. In the sentence I quoted from Richard Wilbur's article, the word *allegorical* occurs. If we will gloss the term not as Poe would have glossed it, with *Pilgrim's Progress* in mind, but as a medieval or Renaissance exegete might have, with the Scriptures or Dante in mind, we will find ourselves led in the right direction. The "fourfold method of exegesis" of the Middle Ages will not provide detailed instructions on how to approach Poe; his stories as rarely confront us with a neat stratification of meanings—one literal, one moral, one allegorical, one anagogical—as they present only one meaning; yet approaching the tales in the spirit of the "fourfold method" will alert us to the special way in which they operate. We shall not grasp Poe's full accomplishment in fiction until we hear each of the several voices of a tale as at once discrete and part of a harmonious totality. Bernard Shaw said of the tales that "they are not merely stories: they are complete works of art, like prayer carpets."

In the same article, which he contributed to the *Nation* (London) on the centenary of Poe's birth, Shaw evaluated Poe's place as critic and poet:

> He was the greatest journalist critic of his time, placing good European work at sight when the European critics were waiting for somebody to tell them what to say. His poetry is so exquisitely refined that posterity will refuse to believe that it belongs to the same civilization as the glory of Mrs. Julia Ward Howe's lilies or the honest doggerel of Whittier.

That Shaw's estimate of Poe's accomplishments in the three areas of his work is neither unusual nor indefensible will be apparent from the foregoing discussion. And yet we must admit that it surprises, however pleasantly. For the figure Poe makes in our minds has somehow failed to achieve the stature his success as critic, poet, and fiction writer would seem to justify.

Often—perhaps one may say generally—we find that the figure of a major writer looms larger in our imaginations than any or even all of his writings would seem to justify. It is as if his total accomplishment exceeded the sum of his individual accomplishments. This is surely the case with Mark Twain, whose writings, with the exception of *Huckleberry Finn* and a few shorter pieces, are deeply flawed, often tawdry, occasionally mawkish. Yet the monument his works and his life make in our minds towers even above Huck's humble, heroic figure. It is the case again, in however different a way, with Emily Dickinson, whose poems, each a slight and seemingly frail utterance, have become fused in our memory and imagination with her enigmatic yet pellucid letters and her life of solitary, saving sanctity—fused into one artifact of almost insupportable clarity, which we rightly term her Life and Works. And no one is likely to dispute that when we turn to Fenimore Cooper or Walt Whitman we find every individual work in some way disappointing; yet, the works of each man, viewed in the context of his whole canon, acquire a solidity and weight and impress us with their authority, their truth, even their beauty.

It is here that our vision of Poe is deficient. The individual accomplishments somehow fail to constellate. To show that the philosophic ideas Poe articulated in *Eureka* are an essential part of the foundation of his tales, that his aesthetic convictions find expression as much in his poems as in his reviews, and that all his works express the enduring concerns of a complex and compelling writer who is indeed an enigma but is not a freak of nature—these are tasks worthy of our best critical efforts. The essays in this collection are linked by their responsiveness to such imperatives. By various means they strive to reveal the complex integrity of the Life and Works of one of the major figures America has contributed to world literature.

The Philosophy of Composition

by Joseph Wood Krutch

In *PMLA* for June 1921, Professor Killis Campbell published the
results of an extended investigation into the contemporary estimate
of Poe. He shows conclusively that even after the success of "The
Raven" the opinion of Poe's poetry in general was not sufficiently
high to give him a place among the most important poets of the
time, and also that it was rather as a critic than as a writer of fiction that his fame was greatest. "It does not," he adds, "affect the
validity of this assertion to add that Poe was chiefly known as a
fearless and caustic critic rather than a just and discriminating
critic."

A considerable portion of this critical writing has inevitably lost
some of its interest. Though its bulk is greater than that of any
other species of composition which Poe undertook, much of it is
concerned with the minute analysis of novels and poems which have
long ceased, in any real sense, to exist. No living reader cares to
have detailed to him through ten closely printed pages the plot of
Norman Leslie: A Tale of Present Times or to have it pointed out
that Mrs. L. H. Sigourney's poem *Zinzendorff* contains a passage
"much injured by the occurrence of the word 'that' at the com-
mencement of both the sixth and seventh line." Yet the fact that
Poe was known "as a fearless and caustic critic" at a formative period
in American literature when most periodical criticism was as pro-
vincially tolerant as the Poet's Corner of a village newspaper is not
without its significance. And still more important is the additional
fact that scattered here and there through these casual reviews as
well as systematically stated in more extended essays are critical opin-

ions remarkable both for their unorthodoxy at the time when they were uttered and for their relation to a set of literary ideas just then in the process of growth. Today Poe the critic is referred to quite as often as Poe the poet, or Poe the fictionist.

Though he gradually became very much interested in his theories, there is no reason to suppose that Poe had begun with any idea of becoming a critic or that he had any particular training for the exercise of that function. His formal education was early broken off, he had little time for extensive reading, and there is no evidence whatever that his familiarity with general literature was great. Just before he joined the staff of the *Messenger* he was in search of a livelihood, the position which was offered him promised that livelihood, and he undertook to review books as he undertook to discharge whatever other duties were expected of him. Thus he turned critic as many another young man has done, less because he had any particular desire to become one than because book reviewing is a routine occupation for which no particular test of competence is required, and, like most others in his position, Poe did the best he could by displaying such knowledge as he happened to have whenever there was an opportunity and by hiding his ignorance as much as possible.

During the course of about a year he reviewed nearly a hundred books of very miscellaneous character, and while he devoted a good deal of space to rather trivial discussions of syntactical and other defects he developed rapidly his skill in the analysis of general propositions suggested by the work under discussion. He gave an enthusiastic reception to a translation of *I Promessi Sposi,* discussed Defoe in connection with a new edition of *Robinson Crusoe,* was surprisingly impressed by Longstreet's *Georgia Scenes,* and in a long review of Drake's poems drew the first and one of the most interesting of his elaborately maintained analyses, making here the distinction between the fancy displayed in *The Culprit Fay* and genuine imagination.

A supplement to the *Messenger* for July 1836 contains a reply by Poe to the various notices which the magazine had received and shows that in a very brief period what was regarded as a fearlessness bordering upon malicious severity had attracted widespread attention to his work. A remark in the course of the same article to the effect that the editor of a paper which had passed some strictures upon the *Messenger* is probably "the identical gentleman who once sent us from Newbern an unfortunate copy of verses" illustrates that tendency to petty and undignified bickering which Poe so abundantly indulged. The reputation which he had gained at this time was essentially of the sort which followed him to the other magazines in which his critical work appeared. From first to last, respect for him was somewhat discounted by that feeling of irritation which the *enfant terrible* always arouses.

In spite of his merits, it would be absurd to maintain that Poe's criticism did not show the effects of his lack of scholarship and his lack of general cultivation. Obscure names and quotations from foreign languages are scattered over his pages, but they are often, perhaps usually, borrowed from secondary sources; and though his reading, called extensive at the University of Virginia, was doubtless great for a college freshman, he suffered all his life from a sort of temporal provinciality as the result of the fact that both his knowledge and his tastes were largely confined to the works of his own half century and his own language. The English magazines he read extensively, and from them he borrowed much of his "learning," but he always gave the impression of knowing more than he did.

He rarely discusses any examples of the older literature, and when he does so it is generally with the assumption that his own generation has refined upon and improved the methods employed in former times. In this regard as in all others he could support his prejudices with ingenious reasoning, but it is usually impossible not to see in it the defense of an imperfectly cultivated taste. "There is," he says,

about "The Antigone," as well as about all the ancient plays, an insufferable *baldness,* or platitude, the inevitable result of inexperience in Art—but a baldness, nevertheless, which pedantry would force us to believe the result of a studied and supremely artistic simplicity alone. Simplicity is, indeed, a very lofty and very effective feature in all true Art—but *not* the simplicity which we see in the Greek drama. . . . He [the Greek dramatist] did what he could—but that was exceedingly little worth. The profound sense of one or two tragic, or rather melo-dramatic elements (such as the idea of inexorable Destiny) —this sense, gleaming at intervals from out the darkness of the ancient stage, serves, in the imperfection of its development, to show not the dramatic ability, but the dramatic *in*ability of the ancients.

Similarly, in reviewing a volume of old English poetry Poe gave high admiration to Marvell alone, finding in Wotton's famous lines beginning "You meaner beauties of the night" "not one of those higher attributes of Poesy which belong to her under all circumstances and throughout all time" and announcing the general proposition that these older poets are overrated.

It is also especially worth remarking that for one who was generally regarded as iconoclastic, Poe's judgment was in its main outlines strikingly in accordance with the general judgment of the Victorian age. Keats, Shelley, and Coleridge he admired, but he thought Tennyson

> the noblest poet who ever lived—*not* because the impressions he produces are, at *all* times, the most profound—*not* because the poetical excitement which he introduces is, at *all* times the most intense—but because it *is*, at all times, the most ethereal—in other words the most elevating and the most pure. No poet is so little of the earth, earthy.

And though, for reasons which have already been pointed out, he anathematized Carlyle and everything which smacked of transcendentalism, such deviations as he made from the Victorian standard were more likely to be in the direction of the cheaply sentimental than in the direction of the more austere. Because he himself was so little robust in his passions, he thought Burns "a man whose merits at least have been more grossly—more preposterously exaggerated (through a series of purely adventitious circumstances) than those of any man that ever lived upon the earth," while Thomas Hood is on the contrary "one of the noblest" of modern poets and Tom Moore "the most skillful literary artist of his day,—perhaps any day,—a man who stands in the singular and really wonderful predicament of being undervalued on account of the profusion with which he has scattered about him his good things." "The brilliancies on any one page of 'Lalla Rookh' would have sufficed to establish that very reputation which has been in a great measure selfdimmed by the galaxied lustre of the entire book."

Because of his own limitations the whole body of realistic literature was nearly meaningless to Poe, but he was, on the other hand, easily moved to an exaggerated admiration for whatever seemed to him to adumbrate his own particular interest. Thus Dickens is praised for his "ideality" rather than for the qualities generally attributed to him; *Undine* is ranked as one of the supreme achievements of prose fiction; while *Conti the Discarded; with other Tales and Fancies* by a certain Mr. Chorley is declared to bear "no little resemblance to that purest, and most enthralling of fictions 'the Bride of Lammermuir,' " (*sic*) apparently for no other reason than that it contains passages of melodrama in the manner of *The Mysteries of Udolpho* and other works of that character.

Poe's especial weakness was, however, for a sort of milk-and-water prettiness into which he appears to have read a meaning related to that ethereal beauty which it was his own desire to create. His idealization of women caused him to be particularly lenient in judging them, and he is thus led into the most extravagant praise of Mrs. Hemans, Mrs. Landon, and their like. "Mrs. Norton is unquestionably—since the death of Mrs. Hemans—the Queen of English song"; if she had written nothing before

> this volume would have established her claim to be the first of living poetesses; but who that is familiar with the world of song can forget the many gems—rich, and beautiful, and rare—with which she has spangled beforetime her starry crown? . . . The random pieces she has poured forth so divinely at intervals, and which hitherto she has made no effort to preserve, have found their way into the hearts of all who can be touched by the mournful or the beautiful, until her name is cherished alike in the humble cottage and the princely hall.

As for the American sisters of these ladies, he was rarely unable to find in their most abysmally sentimental effusions some "nobility" or especially some "passionate purity" to praise. Men were to be slaughtered, but in women praiseworthy intentions were sufficient defense. Speaking again of Mrs. Norton and Mrs. Hemans he writes:

> Scarcely a page, moreover, occurs in the writings of either which does not bear testimony to woman's sufferings and worth. Yes! while it is the fashion to sneer at the purity of woman's heart, and while a pack of literary debauchees are libelling our mothers and our sisters unopposed, from the ranks of that insulted sex have risen up defenders of its innocence, to shame the heartless slanderers to silence. Hear in what eloquent numbers Mrs. Norton vindicates her sex. . . . God bless her who has written this. The wretches who would rob the sex of their purity of heart and their uncomplaining endurance of

suffering, deserve to die, uncheered by woman's nurture, unwept by woman's tenderness. Such beings are not men: they are *aliquid monstri,* monsters in part.

From the example given it is evident that Poe, although he made various penetrating judgments like [those] embodied in the reviews —especially the first—of Hawthorne, did not have a taste which could be relied upon and that to-day even more than when he wrote there are many of his pronouncements which must seem highly capricious. Moreover, it must be admitted that, in spite of the great stress which he laid upon the necessity for fearless and unprejudiced criticism, he was not himself always above influence. His action in recalling his strictures on Griswold in an effort to patch up their quarrel has already been commented upon, and there are other instances where he changed his opinions in deference to new friendships. To Mrs. Gove Nichols he confessed that need might corrupt him, and according to Mrs. Weiss he said: "You must not judge me by what you find me saying in the magazines. Such expressions of opinion are necessarily modified by a thousand circumstances— the wishes of editors, personal friendships, etc." Yet in spite of all these defects there were reasons why his book-reviewing was of considerable importance.

In the first place he was, especially at the beginning of his career, free from any entangling literary alliances. With the exception of J. P. Kennedy, who had aided him, Poe had no literary friends and hence little reason to do otherwise than speak his mind. He was moreover a Southerner working upon a Southern paper and naturally more inclined than a New Englander would be to rebuke the provinciality of American literature, because to do so cost him no pains to any local pride. If, as has been previously suggested, a natural though not wholly conscious envy inclined him to severity, he was permitted upon most occasions to exercise it and the influence of that severity was generally salutary. Reading him to-day we often feel, as we are bound to feel in reading the reviews of any person of the past who dealt much with the ephemeral literature of his time, that he is more often too lenient than too exigent, since most works lose excellence when seen in the perspective of time; but it was not so that he appeared to his contemporaries. Lowell called him "at once the most discriminating, philosophical, and fearless critic upon imaginative works . . . in America," but he added that Poe "some-

times seems to mistake his phial of prussic acid for his inkstand."
In saying that Lowell seems to have expressed a pretty general
opinion.

In the second place Poe had an ideal of criticism which he was
able to describe even if he could not wholly live up to it, and it is
probable that this ideal was not without considerable influence in
raising the standard of American periodical criticism. Few if any
writers of his time realized as keenly as he did the two opposite but
equally malign tendencies of American literary provinciality, and he
was perpetually setting himself against both. Sometimes he was
scornfully denouncing those who assumed as a matter of course that
any European work was better than any native one, but almost as
often he was ridiculing the misplaced patriotism which felt it necessary to praise home products merely because they happen to be our
own. Just as he endeavored to make his criticism almost purely
aesthetic and, by declaring moral influence no necessary part of the
function of a work of art, to remove one of the extraneous elements
which affect literary judgment, so too he tried to remove another
such extraneous element by asking that literature be judged wholly
on its own merits, without reference to either the servility of the
self-conscious provincial or the obstreperous complacency of the too
ardent patriot.

Influence such as that which Poe may have been supposed to have
upon American criticism is extremely difficult to measure. It is certainly very easy to overestimate the importance of such elaborate and
ostentatious executions as those which he performed upon literary
nonentities who would have died very soon of their own weakness,
and the not infrequent outbursts of personal animosity which he
permitted himself doubtless told against him. To his contemporaries, however, he seemed both original and highly important and
the service which he performed may be assumed to have been considerable. Only certain defects prevented it from being much greater.
Partly because of his temperamental predisposition to admire chiefly
works of a very special sort and partly because of his lack of any
real education, he was never able himself to do what he urged upon
American criticism. He could not confront contemporary works with
the masterpieces of the past and dispassionately judge them by the
standard of world literature. He was, perhaps, potentially a citizen
of the literary world, an inheritor of the entire culture of the past;

at least he implied that the critic of literature should be such a one; but because his was, after all, a mind warped by disease and imperfectly cultivated by education, he was never able to claim that citizenship or to come into that inheritance.

So much, then, may be said of the historical importance of Poe's criticism, but its importance in literature as distinguished from history depends less upon the excellence or the defects of his reviewing than upon the set of principles which he developed to parallel his imaginative writing. This body of doctrine, a moderate aestheticism, has an historical importance of its own, since it set itself squarely against the then prevalent American assumption that literature and piety are twin sisters, and it doubtless played a considerable part in breaking the tyranny of didacticism in American letters. But for the purposes of the present study it must be regarded less in its relation to literary development than in relation to the mind which conceived it.

Before the first of his critiques appeared in the *Messenger* Poe had already begun to produce a new kind of literature, and this fact made it inevitable that, granted the gift of exposition which was his to so striking a degree, he should become a remarkable example of that sort of critic whose function is not primarily judicial. Neither intellectual detachment nor catholicity of taste could be expected of him, but because he had, even when he was least conscious of the fact, his own practice to defend, he was bound to write with passion; and because of his powers of rationalization he could not but formulate with remarkable clarity the principles which he drew from a consideration of his own works. The creations of his imagination satisfy perfectly his critical theories because the theories were made to fit the works; but there are many worse ways than this inductive one for arriving at generalizations which are at least illuminating.

This body of doctrine, first suggested in a preface to the 1831 volume of poems, developed piecemeal in various critiques, and finally rather completely summarized in "The Philosophy of Composition" and "The Poetic Principle," may be briefly stated as follows:[1]

The world of literature is essentially a hierarchy. At the bottom

---

[1] The references in parentheses are to volume and page of *The Complete Works of Edgar Allan Poe,* edited by James A. Harrison.

are the realistic works based upon "that evil genius of mere matter-of-fact" against whose "grovelling and degrading assumptions" it is the duty of the critic to fight with every weapon in his power (X, 30). The middle ground is occupied by that species of prose tale in which the artist, "having conceived, with deliberate care, a certain unique or single *effect* to be wrought out—combines such events as may best aid him in establishing this preconceived effect" (XI, 108), while at the top stands the true poem.

The tale has a point of superiority even over the poem.

> In fact, while the *rhythm* of this latter is an essential aid in the development of the poet's highest idea—the idea of the Beautiful—the artificialities of this rhythm are an inseparable bar to the development of all points of thought or expression which have their basis in *Truth*. But Truth is often, and in a very great degree, the aim of the tale. Some of the finest tales are tales of ratiocination. Thus the field of this species of composition, if not in so elevated a region on the mountain of Mind, is a tableland of far vaster extent than the domain of the mere poem. Its products are never so rich, but infinitely more numerous, and more appreciable by the mass of mankind. . . . The author who aims at the purely beautiful in a prose tale is laboring at a great disadvantage. For Beauty can be better treated in the poem. Not so with terror, or passion, or horror, or a multitude of such other points.   (XI, 108-9)

The most exalted species of composition is, however, indisputably that true poetry which may be defined as "The Rhythmical Creation of Beauty" (XIV, 275). From romance it is set off both by the element of rhythm and by the relative vagueness of the incidents with which the emotion is associated, and from a work of science it differs in that it has "for its *immediate* object, pleasure, not truth" (VII, xliii). The most dangerous of the heresies regarding it is "The Heresy of the Didactic" since poetry has nothing to do with either morality or truth, not because these are unimportant but because it is not in the poem that they are best treated. "The world of the mind" is divided into three departments, that of "Pure Intellect," that of "Taste" and that which is occupied by the "Moral Sense."

> Just as the Intellect concerns itself with Truth, so Taste informs us of the Beautiful while the Moral Sense is regardful of Duty. Of this latter, while Conscience teaches the obligation, and Reason the expediency, Taste contents herself with displaying the charms:—wag-

ing war upon Vice solely on the ground of her deformity—her dis-
proportion—her animosity to the fitting, to the appropriate, to the
harmonious—in a word, to Beauty.   (XIV, 273)

Man is born with an instinct for this thing called beauty and in
the world of nature he finds much to satisfy it. "And just as the lily
is repeated in the lake, or the eyes of Amaryllis in the mirror, so is
the mere oral or written repetition of these forms, and sounds, and
colors, and odors, and sentiments, a duplicate source of delight."
Such description is not, however, real poetry because it concerns itself only with the actual and attainable.

He who shall simply sing, with however glowing enthusiasm, or
with however vivid a truth of description, of the sights, and sounds,
and odors, and colours, and sentiments, which greet *him* in common
with all mankind—he, I say, has yet failed to prove his divine title.
There is still a something in the distance which he has been unable
to attain. We have still a thirst unquenchable, to allay which he has
not shown us the crystal springs. This thirst belongs to the immor-
tality of Man. . . . It is the desire of the moth for the star. It is no
mere appreciation of the Beauty before us—but a wild effort to reach
the Beauty above. Inspired by an ecstatic prescience of the glories
beyond the grave, we struggle, by multiform combinations among
the things and thoughts of Time, to attain a portion of that Loveliness whose very elements, perhaps, appertain to eternity alone.
(XIV, 273-74)

Because this Beauty is by definition unrealizable, a certain indefiniteness is one of its attributes and thus "Music is the perfection of
the soul, or idea, of poetry. The *vagueness* of exaltation aroused
by a sweet air (which should be strictly indefinite and never too
strongly suggestive) is precisely what we should aim at in poetry"
(II, 200). "Affectation, within bounds, is . . . no blemish," but since
"ideality" is the supreme attribute of poetry it must never even
when dealing with its chief subject, love, be concerned to any great
extent with passion. "It is precisely this 'unpassionate emotion'
which is the limit of the true poetical art. Passion proper and poesy
are discordant. Poetry, in elevating, tranquilizes the *soul*. With *the
heart* it has nothing to do" (XIII, 131).

This [Poetic] Principle itself is, strictly and simply, the Human As-
piration for Supernal Beauty, the manifestation of the Principle is

always found in *an elevating excitement of the soul*—quite independent of that passion which is the intoxication of the Heart—or of that Truth which is the satisfaction of the Reason. For, in regard to Passion, alas! its tendency is to degrade, rather than to elevate the Soul. Love, on the contrary—Love—the true, the divine Eros—the Uranian, as distinguished from the Dionæan Venus—is unquestionably the purest and truest of all poetical themes.   (XIV, 290)

A poem by Mrs. Amelia Welby which deals with regret over a lost lover is good because

her tone is properly subdued, and is not so much a tone of passion as of a gentle and melancholy regret, interwoven with a pleasant sense of the natural loveliness surrounding the lost in the tomb, and a memory of her human beauty while alive.—Elegiac poems should either assume this character, or dwell purely on the beauty (moral or physical) of the departed—or, better still, utter the notes of triumph. I have endeavored to carry out his latter idea in some verses which I have called "Lenore." . . . A passionate poem is a contradiction in terms.   (XVI, 56)

It is impossible that the soul should remain in this state of elevation for more than a short time. "All high excitements are necessarily transient. Thus a long poem is a paradox. And, without unity of impression, the deepest effects cannot be brought about. Epics were the offspring of an imperfect sense of art" (XI, 107). *Paradise Lost* "is to be regarded as poetical, only when, losing sight of that vital requisite in all works of Art, Unity, we view it merely as a series of minor poems. If, to preserve its Unity—its totality of effect or impression—we read it (as would be necessary) at a single sitting, the result is but a constant alternation of excitement and depression. After a passage of what we feel to be true poetry, there follows, inevitably, a passage of platitude which no critical pre-judgment can force us to admire; but if, upon completing the work, we read it again; omitting the first book—that is to say, commencing with the second—we shall be surprised at now finding that admirable which we before condemned—that damnable which we had previously so much admired. . . . But the day of these artistic anomalies is over. If, at any time, any very long poem *were* popular in reality, which I doubt, it is at least clear that no very long poem will ever be popular again." To praise a poet for "sustained effort" is to be guilty of a vulgar error comparable to that of attempting to estimate "Lamartine by the cubic foot, or Pollok by the pound" (XIV, 267-68). Finally, "all experience has shown" that in the highest manifestations of Beauty the "tone is one of *sadness*. Beauty of whatever kind, in its supreme development, invariably excites the sensitive soul to tears. Melancholy is thus the most legitimate of all the poetic tones" (XIV, 198). "This certain taint of sadness is inseparably connected with all the higher manifestations of true Beauty" (XIV, 279), and

> When music affects us to tears, seemingly causeless, we weep *not*, as Gravina supposes, from "excess of pleasure"; but through excess of an impatient, petulant sorrow that, as mere mortals, we are as yet in no condition to banquet upon those supernal ecstasies of which the music affords us merely a suggestive and indefinite glimpse.   (XVI, 6)

As a result of this analysis of the attributes of supreme beauty it should be possible to discover one subject which satisfies more completely than any other all the requirements, and such is indeed the case.

> Now, never losing sight of the object *supremeness*, or perfection, at all points, I asked myself—"Of all melancholy topics, what, according to the *universal* understanding of mankind, is the *most* melancholy?" Death—was the obvious reply. "And when," I said, "is this most melancholy of topics most poetical?" From what I have already explained at some length, the answer, here also is obvious—"When it most closely allies itself to *Beauty*": the death, then, of a beautiful woman, is, unquestionably, the most poetical topic in the world." (XIV, 201)

In considering this body of doctrine, one cannot but be struck, first of all, by the remarkable appearance of logical completeness which it presents, for once its premises are granted the conclusions are drawn with the same elaborate clarity which is characteristic of Poe's ratiocinative tales. In the second place, it is evident that they do contain certain elements of truth. The definition of Beauty does at least describe very clearly a kind of beauty, and thus though the doctrines may not have the universality claimed for them, they do succeed in doing in their own way all that the best set of critical principles has ever done, which is, not to lay down the laws which govern all art, but to define, as accurately as is possible, a style. Yet it is certainly a work of supererogation to point out that this definition is merely a description of the effect which Poe himself was endeavoring to produce, and since his art was the result of an unrecognized and uncontrollable need, it must follow that the criticism is, like the thing criticised, the product not of the abstract reason of which Poe was so proud but of the forces which led him into a system of rationalization which became ever more complex.

The sources of his criticism have been frequently discussed. It has often been stated that his master was Coleridge and the statement is true—in so far as he had any master except himself. Thus in the preface to the 1831 volume the central doctrine was expressed as follows: "A poem, in my opinion, is opposed to a work of science by having, for its *immediate* object, pleasure, not truth." If we compare this with the statement of Coleridge that "A poem is that species of composition which is opposed to works of science, by proposing for its immediate object not truth," it will appear that Poe's only contribution is to be found in the phrase "in my opinion." Yet it is not to be supposed that the youthful poet, after a thorough course of study in aesthetics, had decided to make his works conform to the theories of Coleridge. Nothing is more characteristic of his mind than the pertinacity with which he held to a useful phrase or a fact upon which he had chanced to fall, and he needed no more than a hint such as he got in this sentence from Coleridge or in Bacon's dictum concerning beauty and strangeness to set him off upon a line of thought which led him through numerous bypaths until it seemed to cover the universe. Coleridge's remark was true because there was need to defend his nonmoral art in a country where literature was generally considered the handmaiden of utilitarian ethics, just as Bacon's was true because the beauty which Poe himself created had always that element of strangeness. Taking the two together he could prove that his own work was pure and perfect, and the hidden spring of energy behind his critical writing was the desire to do just that.

What had been said of the central principle of his aesthetic may be said with equal truth of all its details. It may be, as has been suggested, that his idea of brevity as essential to a true poem was taken from Schlegel, but the fact, vouched for by Mrs. Weiss, that he was himself incapable of sustained effort is surely of more significance in accounting for the existence of the idea than any German source whatsoever. So too his assertion that the highest beauty is always passionless and always melancholy is less the result of a logi-

cal deduction than of the fact that to him passion was always repel-
lent and the highest pleasure shadowed by sadness. Because he did
not himself realize what it was that he sought, a vagueness like music
is inseparable from the highest poetry, and, finally and most specifically, because only unattainable women could move without mad-
dening him, "The most poetic of all ideas is the death of a beautiful woman."

Poe's criticism is, then, as intensely personal as his poetry or his
fiction. Beauty as he defines it includes nothing except beauty of the
sort which he himself produced. And the primary value of the criticism is as an interpretation, not of literature in general, but of his
own works.

It must be remembered, moreover, that however true this interpretation may be upon the level of art it is upon the level of psychology either false or at least misleading. The logic with which he
supports his principles is not the product of a free mind but an
elaborate rationalization whose real function is to support a pre-
determined taste; the character of the satisfaction which his contemplation of "the beautiful" produces is not such as he sees it and
describes it—a sort of intimation of that beauty which lies beyond
human apprehension—but instead a balm to wounded nerves; and
while he is related to those French decadents who acknowledge to
a greater extent than he does the psychological meaning of their
temperaments, he creates for his works a different significance by
inventing an aesthetic which assigns to them new values. Thus his
criticism is not only an analysis of his own work but an analysis
made by one who did not fully understand the genesis of the thing
analyzed and was unconsciously eager to disguise its origin from
himself as well as from others.

The test of practice proves, what the circumstances of its origin
would lead one to expect, that Poe's doctrine can have no standing
as a comprehensive theory of aesthetic. It would exclude too much
from the body of world literature and it would discount too much
of major importance, while it exalts minor works to a pre-eminence
which they could have only for those whose temperament was somehow abnormal like his. Judged by his principles the *Odyssey* would
be, as Andrew Lang points out, inferior to "Ulalume," and *Le
Festin de Pierre* to *Undine*. Moreover, since Poe's banishment of
morality from art is not merely a protest against didacticism but im-

plies also that even as *themes,* moral ideas must be excluded, it follows that all works of the highest art must be, like his own, very remote from human life. As Lang said in another essay:

> To any one who believes that the best, the immortal poetry, is nobly busied with great actions and great passion, Poe's theory seems fatally narrow. Without the conceptions of duty and truth we can have no *Antigone* and no *Prometheus.* The great and paramount ideas have always been the inspirers of honorable actions, and by following them men and women are led into the dramatic situations which are the materials of Shakespeare. Aeschylus, and Homer. There is an immortal strength in the stories of great actions, but Poe in theory and practice disdains all action and rejects this root of immortality. He deliberately chooses fantasy for his portion. Now, while it is not the business of poetry to go about distributing tracts, she can never neglect actions and situations which under her spell become unconscious lessons of morality.

And this is essentially true, even though one does not demand that poetry should inculcate even "unconscious lessons of morality," since moral ideas, true or false, are the source of many of the most exalted passions which poetry can utilize.

. . . .

We have, then, traced Poe's art to an abnormal condition of the nerves and his critical ideas to a rationalized defense of the limitations of his own taste. We have also indicated that even as an interpretation of his own works his criticism falls short of psychological truth and it might seem that we had thus undertaken to destroy the value of his work. Such is far, however, from being the intention. The question whether or not the case of Poe represents an exaggerated example of the process by which all creation is performed is at least an open question. The extent to which all imaginative works are the result of the unfulfilled desires which spring from either idiosyncratic or universally human maladjustments to life is only beginning to be investigated, and with it is linked the related question of the extent to which all critical principles are at bottom the systematized and rationalized expression of instinctive tastes which are conditioned by causes often unknown to those whom they affect. The problem of finding an answer to these questions and of determining what effect, if any, the findings in any particular case should have upon the evaluation of the works of imagination or interpretation so produced, is the one distinctly new problem which the critic of today is called upon to consider. He must, in a word, endeavor to find the relationship which exists between psychology and aesthetics, but since the present state of knowledge is not such as to enable anyone satisfactorily to determine that relationship, we must proceed only with the greatest caution and content ourselves with saying that the fallacy of origins, that species of false logic by which a thing is identified with its ultimate source, is nowhere more dangerous than in the realm of art, and criticism is, at times at least, much more of an art than a science.

Whatever a critic can convincingly read into a work may be said to be actually there, even though it be thought of as the creation of the critic rather than of the author criticised. And the works of Poe have his own interpretations of them as one of the various modes in which they exist. They have been read in the light of his intention and the effect which they have produced has been at least so modified by that intention as to be different from the effect which they would have produced had he and his readers been aware of the psychological processes behind them. That legend of himself which he fashioned in a manner so marvelously inclusive that it employs as material everything from the events of his daily life to the products of his imagination is finally completed by his interpretation. His criticism inscribes a curve within which everything else is included; it unifies all the various aspects of his life and work; and thus it makes his legend as a whole, rather than any of the individual stories or poems which are but a part of it, his supreme artistic creation.

From "Vulgarity in Literature"

by Aldous Huxley

Eulalie, Ulalume, Raven and Bells, Conqueror Worm and Haunted Palace. . . . Was Edgar Allan Poe a major poet? It would surely never occur to any English-speaking critic to say so. And yet, in France, from 1850 till the present time, the best poets of each generation—yes, and the best critics, too; for, like most excellent poets, Baudelaire, Mallarmé, Paul Valéry are also admirable critics —have gone out of their way to praise him. Only a year or two ago M. Valéry repeated the now traditional French encomium of Poe, and added at the same time a protest against the faintness of our English praise. We who are speakers of English and not English scholars, who were born into the language and from childhood have been pickled in its literature—we can only say, with all due respect, that Baudelaire, Mallarmé and Valéry are wrong and that Poe is not one of our major poets. A taint of vulgarity spoils, for the English reader, all but two or three of his poems—the marvellous "City in the Sea" and "To Helen," for example, whose beauty and crystal perfection make us realize, as we read them, what a very great artist perished on most of the occasions when Poe wrote verse. It is to this perished artist that the French poets pay their tribute. Not being English, they are incapable of appreciating those finer shades of vulgarity that ruin Poe for us, just as we, not being French, are incapable of appreciating those finer shades of lyrical beauty which are, for them, the making of La Fontaine.

The substance of Poe is refined; it is his form that is vulgar. He is, as it were, one of Nature's Gentlemen, unhappily cursed with incorrigible bad taste. To the most sensitive and high-souled man in

Part VI of "Vulgarity in Literature" by Aldous Huxley. From *Music at Night and Other Essays*. © 1930, 1958 by Aldous Huxley. Reprinted by permission of Mrs. Laura Huxley, Harper & Row, Publishers, and Chatto & Windus Ltd.

the world we should find it hard to forgive, shall we say, the wearing of a diamond ring on every finger. Poe does the equivalent of this in his poetry; we notice the solecism and shudder. Foreign observers do not notice it; they detect only the native gentlemanliness in the poetical intention, not the vulgarity in the details of execution. To them, we seem perversely and quite incomprehensibly unjust.

It is when Poe tries to make it too poetical that his poetry takes on its peculiar tinge of badness. Protesting too much that he is a gentleman, and opulent into the bargain, he falls into vulgarity. Diamond rings on every finger proclaim the parvenu.

Consider, for example, the first two stanzas of "Ulalume."

> The skies they were ashen and sober;
>   The leaves they were crisped and sere—
>   The leaves they were withering and sere:
> It was night in the lonesome October
>   Of my most immemorial year:
> It was hard by the dim lake of Auber,
>   In the misty mid region of Weir:—
> It was down by the dank tarn of Auber,
>   In the ghoul-haunted woodland of Weir.
>
> Here once, through an alley Titanic,
>   Of cypress, I roamed with my Soul—
>   Of cypress, with Psyche, my Soul.
> These were days when my heart was volcanic
>   As the scoriac rivers that roll—
>   As the lavas that restlessly roll
> Their sulphurous currents down Yaanek,
>   In the ultimate climes of the Pole—
> That groan as they roll down Mount Yaanek,
>   In the realms of the Boreal Pole.

These lines protest too much (and with what a variety of voices!) that they are poetical, and, protesting, are therefore vulgar. To start with, the walloping dactylic metre is all too musical. Poetry ought to be musical, but musical with tact, subtly and variously. Metres whose rhythms, as in this case, are strong, insistent and practically invariable offer the poet a kind of short cut to musicality. They provide him (my subject calls for a mixture of metaphors) with a ready-made, reach-me-down music. He does not have to create a music appropriately modulated to his meaning; all he has to do is to shovel the meaning into the moving stream of the metre and allow the current to carry it along on waves that, like those of the best hairdressers, are guaranteed permanent. Many nineteenth century poets used these metrical short cuts to music, with artistically fatal results.

> Then when nature around me is smiling
> The last smile which answers to mine,
> I do not believe it beguiling,
> Because it reminds me of thine.

How can one take even Byron seriously, when he protests his musicalness in such loud and vulgar accents? It is only by luck or an almost super-human poetical skill that these all too musical metres can be made to sound, through their insistent barrel-organ rhythms, the intricate, personal music of the poet's own meaning. Byron occasionally, for a line or two, takes the hard kink out of those dactylic permanent waves and appears, so to speak, in his own musical hair; and Hood, by an unparalleled prodigy of technique, turns even the reach-me-down music of "The Bridge of Sighs" into a personal music, made to the measure of the subject and his own emotion. Moore, on the contrary, is always perfectly content with the permanent wave; and Swinburne, that super-Moore of a later generation, was also content to be a permanent waver—the most accomplished, perhaps, in all the history of literature. The complexity of his ready-made musics and his technical skill in varying the number, shape and contour of his permanent waves are simply astonishing. But, like Poe and the others, he protested too much, he tried to be too poetical. However elaborately devious his short cuts to music may be, they are still short cuts—and short cuts (this is the irony) to poetical vulgarity.

A quotation and a parody will illustrate the difference between ready-made music and music made to measure. I remember (I trust correctly) a simile of Milton's:

> Like that fair field
> Of Enna, where Proserpine gathering flowers,
> Herself a fairer flower, by gloomy Dis
> Was gathered, which cost Ceres all that pain
> To seek her through the world.

Rearranged according to their musical phrasing, these lines would have to be written thus:

> Like that fair field of Enna,
>   where Proserpine gathering flowers,
> Herself a fairer flower,
>   by gloomy Dis was gathered,
> Which cost Ceres all that pain
> To seek her through the world.

The contrast between the lyrical swiftness of the first four phrases, with that row of limping spondees which tells of Ceres' pain, is thrillingly appropriate. Bespoke, the music fits the sense like a glove.

How would Poe have written on the same theme? I have ventured to invent his opening stanza.

> It was noon in the fair field of Enna,
>   When Proserpina gathering flowers—
> Herself the most fragrant of flowers,
> Was gathered away to Gehenna
>   By the Prince of Plutonian powers;
> Was borne down the windings of Brenner
>   To the gloom of his amorous bowers—
> Down the tortuous highway of Brenner
>   To the God's agapemonous bowers.

The parody is not too outrageous to be critically beside the point; and anyhow the music is genuine Poe. That permanent wave is unquestionably an *ondulation de chez Edgar.* The much too musical metre is (to change the metaphor once more) like a rich chasuble, so stiff with gold and gems that it stands unsupported, a carapace of jewelled sound, into which the sense, like some snotty little seminarist, irrelevantly creeps and is lost. This music of Poe's—how much less really musical it is than that which, out of his nearly neutral decasyllables, Milton fashioned on purpose to fit the slender beauty of Proserpine, the strength and swiftness of the ravisher and her mother's heavy, despairing sorrow!

Of the versification of "The Raven" Poe says, in his "Philosophy of Composition":

My first object (as usual) was originality. The extent to which this has been neglected, in versification, is one of the most unaccountable things in the world. Admitting that there is little possibility of variety in mere *rhythm,* it is still clear that the possible varieties of metre and stanza are absolutely infinite—and yet, *for centuries, no man, in verse, has ever done, or ever seemed to think of doing, an original thing.*

This fact, which Poe hardly exaggerates, speaks volumes for the good sense of the poets. Feeling that almost all strikingly original metres and stanzas were only illegitimate short cuts to a music which, when reached, turned out to be but a poor and vulgar substitute for individual music, they wisely stuck to the less blatantly musical metres of tradition. The ordinary iambic decasyllable, for example, is intrinsically musical enough to be just able, when required, to stand up by itself. But its musical stiffness can easily be taken out of it. It can be now a chasuble, a golden carapace of sound, now, if the poet so desires, a pliant, soft and, musically speaking, almost neutral material, out of which he can fashion a special music of his own to fit his thoughts and feelings in all their incessant transformations. Good landscape painters seldom choose a "picturesque" subject; they want to paint their own picture, not have it imposed on them by nature. In the thoroughly paintable little places of this world you will generally find only bad painters. (It's so easy to paint the thoroughly paintable.) The good ones prefer the unspectacular neutralities of the Home Counties to those Cornish coves and Ligurian fishing villages, whose picturesqueness is the delight of all those who have no pictures of their own to project on to the canvas. It is the same with poetry: good poets avoid what I may call, by analogy, "musicesque" metres, preferring to create their own music out of raw materials as nearly as possible neutral. Only bad poets, or good poets against their better judgment, and by mistake, go to the Musicesque for their material. "For centuries no man, in verse, has ever done, or ever seemed to think of doing, an original thing." It remained for Poe and the other nineteenth century metrists to do it; Procrustes-like, they tortured and amputated significance into fitting the ready-made music of their highly original metres and stanzas. The result was, in most cases, as vulgar as a Royal Academy Sunrise on Ben Nevis (with Highland Cattle) or a genuine hand-painted sketch of Portofino.

How could a judge so fastidious as Baudelaire listen to Poe's music and remain unaware of its vulgarity? A happy ignorance of English versification preserved him, I fancy, from this realization. His own imitations of mediaeval hymns prove how far he was from understanding the first principles of versification in a language where the stresses are not, as in French, equal, but essentially and insistently uneven. In his Latin poems Baudelaire makes the ghost of Bernard of Cluny write as though he had learned his art from Racine. The principles of English versification are much the same as those of mediaeval Latin. If Baudelaire could discover lines composed of equally stressed syllables in Bernard, he must also have discovered them in Poe. Interpreted according to Racinian principles, such verses as

> It was down by the dank tarn of Auber,
> In the ghoul-haunted woodland of Weir

must have taken on, for Baudelaire, heaven knows what exotic subtlety of rhythm. We can never hope to guess what that ghoul-haunted woodland means to a Frenchman possessing only a distant and theoretical knowledge of our language.

Returning now to "Ulalume," we find that its too poetical metre has the effect of vulgarizing by contagion what would be otherwise perfectly harmless and refined technical devices. Thus, even the very mild alliterations in "the ghoul-haunted woodland of Weir" seem to protest too much. And yet an iambic verse beginning "Woodland of Weir, ghoul-haunted," would not sound in the least over-poetical. It is only in the dactylic environment that those two w's strike one as protesting too much.

And then there are the proper names. Well used, proper names can be relied on to produce the most thrilling musical-magical effects. But use them without discretion, and the magic evaporates into abracadabrical absurdity, or becomes its own mocking parody; the over-emphatic music shrills first into vulgarity and finally into ridiculousness. Poe tends to place his proper names in the most conspicuous position in the line (he uses them constantly as rhyme words), showing them off—these magical-musical jewels—as the *rastacouaire* might display the twin cabochon emeralds at his shirt cuffs and the platinum wrist watch, with his monogram in diamonds. These proper-name rhyme-jewels are particularly flashy in Poe's case because they are mostly dissyllabic. Now, the dissyllabic rhyme in English is poetically so precious and so conspicuous by its richness that, if it is not perfect in itself and perfectly used, it emphatically ruins what it was meant emphatically to adorn. Thus, sound and association make of "Thule" a musical-magical proper name of exceptional power. But when Poe writes,

> I have reached these lands but newly
> From an ultimate dim Thule,

he spoils the effect which the word ought to produce by insisting too much, and incompetently, on its musicality. He shows off his jewel as conspicuously as he can, but only reveals thereby the badness of its setting and his own Levantine love of display. For "newly" does not rhyme with "Thule"—or only rhymes on condition that you pronounce the adverb as though you were a Bengali, or the name as though you came from Whitechapel. The paramour of Goethe's king rhymed perfectly with the name of his kingdom; and when Laforgue wrote of that "roi de Thulé, Immaculé" his *rime riche* was entirely above suspicion. Poe's rich rhymes, on the contrary, are seldom above suspicion. That dank tarn of Auber is only very dubiously a fit poetical companion for the tenth month, and though Mount Yaanek is, *ex hypothesi*, a volcano, the rhyme with volcanic is, frankly, impossible. On other occasions Poe's proper names rhyme not only well enough, but actually, in the particular context, much too well. Dead D'Elormie, in "The Bridal Ballad," is prosodically in order, because Poe had brought his ancestors over with the Conqueror (as he also imported the ancestors of that Guy de Vere who wept his tear over Lenore) for the express purpose of providing a richly musical-magical rhyme to "bore me" and "before me." Dead D'Elormie is first cousin to Edward Lear's aged Uncle Arly, sitting on a heap of Barley—ludicrous; but also (unlike dear Uncle Arly) horribly vulgar, because of the too musical lusciousness of his invented name and his display, in all tragical seriousness, of an obviously faked Norman pedigree. Dead D'Elormie is a poetical disaster.

Our Cousin, Mr. Poe

by *Allen Tate*

When I was about fourteen there were in our house, along with the novels of John Esten Cooke, E. P. Roe, and Augusta Evans, three small volumes of Edgar Allan Poe. That, by my reckoning, was a long time ago. Even then the books were old and worn, whether from use (I suppose not) or from neglect, it did not occur to me to enquire. I remember, or imagine I remember the binding, which was blue, and the size, which was small, and the paper, which was yellow and very thin. One volume contained the Poems, prefaced by Lowell's famous "biography." In this volume I am sure, for I read it more than the others, was the well-known, desperate, and asymmetrical photograph, which I gazed at by the hour and which I hoped that I should some day resemble. Another volume contained most, or at least the most famous of the Tales: "Ligeia," which I liked best (I learned in due time that Poe had, too); "Morella" and "William Wilson," which I now like best; and "The Fall of the House of Usher," which was a little spoiled for me even at fourteen by the interjection of the "Mad Tryst of Sir Launcelot Canning." Perhaps it was in this volume that I admired "Marginalia," the first "criticism" I remember reading; but I did not discern either the bogus erudition or the sense of high literature which Poe was the first American to distinguish from entertainment and self-improvement through books; the merits as well as the defects went over my head. "Marginalia" could not at any rate have been in the third volume, which was given to a single long work: *Eureka—A Prose Poem*. This astrophilosophical discourse, which the late Paul Valéry took more seriously than any English or American critic ever did,

"Our Cousin, Mr. Poe" by Allen Tate. Address delivered before the Poe Society of Baltimore on the centenary of his death, October 7, 1949; and repeated as a Bergen Lecture at Yale University, November 14, 1949. From *Collected Essays*. © 1960 by Allen Tate. Reprinted by permission of the publisher, Alan Swallow.

fell in with my readings in popular astronomical books. In the back-yard I arranged in a straight line peas, cherries, and oranges, in the proportionate sizes and distances of the sun and planets, and some hundreds of feet away (an inch perhaps to a thousand light-years) an old volley ball of my elder brothers' to represent Alpha Lyrae.

Later, on another occasion, I expect to examine *Eureka* at length, as I read it now, not as I read it at fourteen; yet before I leave it I must mention two other circumstances of my boyhood reading and the feeling that accompanied it. It lives for me as no later experience of ideas lives, because it was the first I had. The "proposition" that Poe undertook to demonstrate has come back to me at intervals in the past thirty-six years with such unpredictable force that now I face it with mingled resignation and dismay. I can write it without looking it up:

> In the original unity of the first thing lies the secondary cause of all things, with the germ of their inevitable annihilation.

This is not the place to try to say what Poe meant by it. I could not, at fourteen, have guessed what it meant even after I had read the book; yet it is a fact of my boyhood (which I cannot suppose unique) that this grandiose formula for cosmic cataclysm became a part of my consciousness through no effort of my own but seemed to come to me like a dream, and came back later, like a nursery rhyme, or a tag from a popular song, unbidden.

The other circumstance I am surer of because it was a visible fact, a signature in faded brown ink on the flyleaf of *Eureka:* it told me years later that the three volumes had been printed earlier than 1870, the year the man who had owned them died. He was my great-grandfather. My mother had said, often enough, or on some occasion that fixed it in memory, that her grandfather had "known Mr. Poe." (She was of the era when all eminent men, living or recently dead, were "Mr.") I knew as a boy that my great-grandfather had been a "poet," and in 1930 I found some of his poems, which I forbear to discuss. He had for a while been editor of the *Alexandria Gazette* at about the time of Mr. Poe's death. Both were "Virginians," though Virginians of somewhat different schools and points of view. I can see my great-grandfather in Poe's description of a preacher who called upon him in the summer of 1848: "He stood smiling and bowing at the madman Poe."

I have brought together these scattered memories of my first reading of a serious writer because in discussing any writer, or in coming to terms with him, we must avoid the trap of mere abstract
evaluation, and try to reproduce the actual conditions of our relation to him. It would be difficult for me to take Poe up, "study"
him, and proceed to a critical judgment. One may give these affairs
the look of method, and thus deceive almost everybody but oneself.
In reading Poe we are not brought up against a large, articulate
scheme of experience, such as we see adumbrated in Hawthorne or
Melville, which we may partly sever from personal association, both
in the writer and in ourselves. Poe surrounds us with Eliot's "wilder-
ness of mirrors," in which we see a subliminal self endlessly repeated
or, turning, a new posture of the same figure. It is not too harsh,
I think, to say that it is stupid to suppose that by "evaluating" this
forlorn demon in the glass, we dispose of him. For Americans, perhaps for most modern men, he is with us like a dejected cousin: we
may "place" him but we may not exclude him from our board. This
is the recognition of a relationship, almost of the blood, which we
must in honor acknowledge: what destroyed him is potentially destructive of us. Not only this; we must acknowledge another obligation, if, like most men of my generation, we were brought up in
houses where the works of Poe took their easy place on the shelf
with the family Shakespeare and the early novels of Ellen Glasgow.
This is the obligation of loyalty to one's experience: he was in our
lives and we cannot pretend that he was not. Not even Poe's great
power in Europe is quite so indicative of his peculiar "place" as
his unquestioned, if unexamined, acceptance among ordinary gentle
people whose literary culture was not highly developed. The horrors
of Poe created not a tremor in the bosoms of young ladies or a
moment's anxiety in the eyes of vigilant mothers. I suppose the
gentlemen of the South did not read him much after his time; in
his time, they could scarcely have got the full sweep and depth of
the horror. Nothing that Mr. Poe wrote, it was said soon after his
death, could bring a blush to the cheek of the purest maiden.

But I doubt that maidens read very far in the Tales. If they had
they would have found nothing to disconcert the image that Miss
Susan Ingram recorded from a visit of Poe to her family a few
weeks before his death:

Although I was only a slip of a girl and he what seemed to me then quite an old man, and a great literary one at that, we got on together beautifully. He was one of the most courteous gentlemen I have ever seen, and that gave great charm to his manner. None of his pictures that I have ever seen look like the picture of Poe that I keep in my memory . . . there was something in his face that is in none of them. Perhaps it was in the eyes.

If he was a madman he was also a gentleman. Whether or not we accept Mr. Krutch's theory,[1] we know, as this sensible young lady knew, that she was quite safe with him. A gentleman? Well, his manners were exemplary (when he was not drinking) and to the casual eye at any rate his exalted idealization of Woman (even of some very foolish women) was only a little more humorless, because more intense, than the standard cult of Female Purity in the Old South.

What Mr. Poe on his own had done with the cult it was not possible then to know. A gentleman and a Southerner, he was not quite, perhaps, a Southern gentleman. The lofty intellect of Ligeia, of Madeline, of Berenice, or of Eleanora, had little utility in the social and economic structure of Virginia, which had to be perpetuated through the issue of the female body, while the intellect, which was public and political, remained under the supervision of the gentlemen. Although Morella had a child (Poe's only heroine, I believe, to be so compromised), she was scarcely better equipped than Virginia Clemm herself to sustain more than the immaculate half of the vocation of the Southern lady. "But the fires," writes Morella's narrator-husband, "were not of Eros." And we know, at the end of the story, that the daughter is no real daughter but, as Morella's empty "tomb" reveals, Morella herself come back as a vampire to wreak upon her "lover" the vengeance due him. Why is it due him? Because, quite plainly, the lover lacked, as he always lacked with his other heroines, the "fires of Eros." The soul of Morella's husband "burns with fires it had never before known . . . and bitter and tormenting to my spirit was the gradual conviction that I could in no manner define their unusual meaning, or regulate their vague intensity." Perhaps in the soul of John Randolph alone

[1] The theory that Poe was sexually impotent.

of Virginia gentlemen strange fires burned. The fires that were not of Eros were generally for the land and oratory, and the two fires were predictably regulated.

Poe's strange fire is his leading visual symbol, but there is not space in an essay to list all its appearances. You will see it in the eye of the Raven; in "an eye large, liquid, and luminous beyond comparison," of Roderick Usher; in the burning eye of the old man in "The Tell-Tale Heart"; in "Those eyes! those large, those shining, those divine orbs," of the Lady Ligeia. Poe's heroes and heroines are always burning with a hard, gemlike flame—a bodyless exaltation of spirit that Poe himself seems to have carried into the drawing room, where its limited visibility was sufficient guarantee of gentlemanly behavior. But privately, and thus, for him, publicly, in his stories, he could not "regulate its vague intensity."

I cannot go into this mystery here as fully as I should like; yet I may, I think, ask a question: Why did not Poe use explicitly the universal legend of the vampire? Perhaps some instinct for aesthetic distance made him recoil from it; perhaps the literal, businesslike way the vampire went about making its living revolted the "ideality" of Poe. At any rate D. H. Lawrence was no doubt right in describing as vampires his women characters; the men, soon to join them as "undead," have by some defect of the moral will, made them so.

The mysterious exaltation of spirit which is invariably the unique distinction of his heroes and heroines is not quite, as I have represented it, bodyless. *It inhabits a human body but that body is dead. The spirits prey upon one another with destructive fire which is at once pure of lust and infernal.* All Poe's characters represent one degree or another in a movement towards an archetypal condition: the survival of the soul in a dead body; but only in "The Facts in the Case of Monsieur Valdemar" is the obsessive subject explicit.

In none of the nineteenth century comment on "The Fall of the House of Usher" that I have read, and in none of our own period, is there a feeling of shock, or even of surprise, that Roderick Usher is in love with his sister: the relation not being physical, it is "pure." R. H. Stoddard, the least sympathetic of the serious early biographers, disliked Poe's morbidity, but admitted his purity. The American case against Poe, until the first World War, rested upon his moral indifference, or his limited moral range. The range is limited, but there is no indifference; there is rather a compulsive, even a profound, interest in a moral problem of universal concern. His contemporaries could see in the love stories neither the incestuous theme nor what it meant, because it was not represented literally. The theme and its meaning as I see them are unmistakable: the symbolic compulsion that drives through, and beyond, physical incest moves towards the extinction of the beloved's will in complete possession, not of her body, but of her being; there is the reciprocal force, returning upon the lover, of self-destruction. Lawrence shrewdly perceived the significance of Poe's obsession with incestuous love. Two persons of the least dissimilarity offer the least physical resistance to mutual participation in the *fire* of a common being. Poe's most casual reader perceives that his lovers never do anything but contemplate each other, or pore upon the rigmarole of preposterously erudite, ancient books, most of which never existed. They are living in each other's insides, in the hollows of which burns the fire of will and intellect.

The fire is a double symbol; it lights and it burns. It is overtly the "light" of reason but as action it becomes the consuming fire of the abstract intellect, without moral significance, which invades the being of the beloved. It is the fire that, having illuminated, next destroys. Lawrence is again right in singling out for the burden of his insight the epigraph to "Ligeia," which Poe had quoted from Glanvill: "Man does not yield himself to the angels, nor unto death utterly, save through the weakness of his own feeble will." Why do these women of monstrous will and intellect turn into vampires? Because, according to Lawrence, the lovers have not subdued them through the body to the biological level, at which sanity alone is possible, and they retaliate by devouring their men. This view is perhaps only partly right. I suspect that the destruction works both ways, that the typical situation in Poe is more complex than Lawrence's version of it.

If we glance at "The Fall of the House of Usher" we shall be struck by a singular feature of the catastrophe. Bear in mind that Roderick and Madeline are brother and sister, and that the standard hyperaesthesia of the Poe hero acquires in Roderick a sharper reality than in any of the others, except perhaps William Wilson. His naked sensitivity to sound and light is not "regulated" to the forms of the human situation; it is a mechanism operating apart from the moral consciousness. We have here something like a capacity for mere sensation, as distinguished from sensibility, which in Usher is atrophied. In terms of the small distinction that I am offering here, sensibility keeps us in the world; sensation locks us into the self, feeding upon the disintegration of its objects and absorbing them into the void of the ego. The lover, circumventing the body into the secret being of the beloved, tries to convert the spiritual object into an object of sensation: the intellect which knows and the will which possesses are unnaturally turned upon that centre of the beloved which should remain inviolate.

As the story of Usher opens, the Lady Madeline is suffering from a strange illness. She dies. Her brother has, of course, possessed her inner being, and killed her; or thinks he has, or at any rate wishes to think that she is dead. This is all a little vague: perhaps he has deliberately entombed her alive, so that she will die by suffocation —a symbolic action for extinction of being. Why has he committed this monstrous crime? Sister though she is, she is nevertheless not entirely identical with him: she has her own otherness, of however slight degree, resisting his hypertrophied will. He puts her alive, though "cataleptic," into the "tomb." (Poe never uses graves, only tombs, except in "Premature Burial." His corpses, being half dead, are thus only half buried; they rise and walk again.) After some days Madeline breaks out of the tomb and confronts her brother in her bloody cerements. This is the way Poe presents the scene:

> ". . . Is she not hurrying to upbraid me for my haste? Have I not heard her footsteps on the stair? Do I not distinguish the heavy and horrible beating of her heart? *Madman!*"—here he sprang furiously to his feet, and shrieked out his syllables, as if in his effort he were giving up his soul—"*Madman! I tell you that she now stands without the door!*"

> As if in the superhuman energy of his utterance there had been found the potency of a spell—the huge antique panels to which the speaker pointed threw slowly back, upon the instant, their ponderous and ebony jaws. It was the work of the rushing gust—but then without those doors there *did* stand the lofty and enshrouded figure of the lady Madeline of Usher. There was blood upon her white robes, and the evidence of some bitter struggle upon every portion of her emaciated frame. For a moment she remained trembling and reeling to and fro upon the threshold, then, with a low moaning cry, fell heavily inward upon the person of her brother, and in her violent

and now final death-agonies, bore him to the floor a corpse, and a victim to the terrors he had anticipated.

Madeline, back from the tomb, neither dead nor alive, is in the middle state of the unquiet spirit of the vampire, whose heartbeats are "heavy and horrible." There is no evidence that Poe knew any anthropology; yet in some legends of vampirism the undead has a sluggish pulse, or none at all. In falling prone upon her brother she takes the position of the vampire suffocating its victim in a sexual embrace. By these observations I do not suggest that Poe was conscious of what he was doing; had he been, he might have done it even worse. I am not saying, in other words, that Poe is offering us, in the Lady Madeline, a vampire according to Bram Stoker's specifications. An imagination of any power at all will often project its deepest assumptions about life in symbols that duplicate, without the artist's knowledge, certain meanings, the origins of which are sometimes as old as the race. If a writer ambiguously exalts the "spirit" over the "body," and the spirit must live wholly upon another spirit, some version of the vampire legend is likely to issue as the symbolic situation.

Although the action is reported by a narrator, the fictional point of view is that of Usher: it is all seen through his eyes. But has Madeline herself not also been moving towards the cataclysmic end in the enveloping action outside the frame of the story? Has not her *will to know* done its reciprocal work upon the inner being of her brother? Their very birth had violated their unity of being. They must achieve spiritual identity in mutual destruction. The physical symbolism of the fissured house, of the miasmic air, and of the special order of nature surrounding the House of Usher and conforming to the laws of the spirits inhabiting it—all this supports the central dramatic situation, which moves towards spiritual unity through disintegration.

> In the original unity of the first thing lies the secondary cause of all things, with the germ of their inevitable annihilation.

Repeated here, in the context of the recurrent subject of the Tales, the thesis of *Eureka* has a sufficient meaning and acquires something of the dignity that Valéry attributed to it. Professor Quinn adduces quotations from mathematical physicists to prove that Poe, in *Eureka,* was a prophet of science. It is a subject on which I am not entitled to an opinion. But even if Professor Quinn is right, the claim is irrelevant, and is only another version of the attempt today to make religion and the arts respectable by showing that they are semi-scientific. Another sort of conjecture seems to me more profitable: that in the history of the moral imagination in the nineteenth century Poe occupies a special place. No other writer in England or the United States, or, so far as I know, in France, went so far as Poe in his vision of dehumanized man.

His characters are, in the words of William Wilson's double, "dead to the world"; they are machines of sensation and will, with correspondences, in the physical universe, to particles and energy. Poe's engrossing obsession in *Eureka* with the cosmic destiny of man issued in a quasi-cosmology, a more suitable extension of his vision than any mythology, homemade or traditional, could have offered him. The great mythologies are populous worlds, but a cosmology need have nobody in it. In Poe's, the hyperaesthetic egoist has put all other men into his void: he is alone in the world, and thus dead to it. If we place Poe against the complete Christian imagination of Dante, whom he resembles in his insistence upon a cosmic extension of the moral predicament, the limits of his range are apparent, and the extent of his insight within those limits. The quality of Poe's imagination can be located, as I see it, in only two places in Dante's entire scheme of the after-life: Cantos XIII and XXXII of the *Inferno.* In Canto XIII, the Harpies feed upon the living trees enclosing the shades of suicides—those "violent against themselves," who will not resume their bodies at the Resurrection, for "man may not have what he takes from himself." In XXXII, we are in Caïna, the ninth circle, where traitors to their kin lie half buried in ice, up to the pubic shadow—"where the doleful shades were . . . sounding with their teeth like storks." Unmotivated treachery, for the mere intent of injury, and self-violence are Poe's obsessive subjects. He has neither Purgatory nor Heaven; and only two stations in Hell.

Let us turn briefly to the question of Poe's style. He has several styles, and it is not possible to damn them all at once. The critical style, which I shall not be able to examine here, is on occasion the best; he is a lucid and dispassionate expositor, he is capable of clear and rigorous logic (even from mistaken premises, as in "The Rationale of Verse"), when he is not warped by envy or the desire to flatter. He is most judicial with his peers, least with his inferiors, whom he either overestimates or wipes out. As for the fictional style, it, too, varies; it is perhaps at its sustained best, in point of sobriety and restraint, in the tales of deduction. Exceptions to this observation are "Descent into the Maelström," "The Narrative of Arthur Gordon Pym," and perhaps one or two others in a genre which stems from the eighteenth century "voyage." These fictions demanded a Defoe-like verisimilitude which was apparently beyond his reach when he dealt with his obsessive theme. Again I must make an exception: "William Wilson," one of the serious stories (by serious, I mean an ample treatment of the obsession), is perspicuous in diction and on the whole credible in realistic detail. I quote a paragraph:

> The extensive enclosure was irregular in form, having many capacious recesses. Of these, three or four of the largest constituted the play-ground. It was level, and covered with fine hard gravel. I well remember it had no trees, nor benches, nor anything similar within it. Of course it was in the rear of the house. In front lay a small parterre, planted with box and other shrubs; but through this sacred division we passed only upon rare occasions indeed—such as a first advent to school or final departure hence, or perhaps, when a parent or a friend having called upon us, we joyfully took our way home for the Christmas or Midsummer holydays.

It is scarcely great prose, but it has an eighteenth century directness, and even elegance, of which Poe was seldom capable in his stories. I surmise that the playground at Dr. Bransby's school at Stoke-Newington, where, as a child, he was enrolled for five years, recalled one of the few periods of his life which he could detach from the disasters of manhood and face with equanimity. Now a part of the description of the Lady Ligeia:

> . . . I examined the contour of the lofty and pale forehead—it was faultless—how cold indeed that word when applied to a majesty so divine!—the skin rivalling the purest ivory, the commanding extent and repose, the gentle prominence of the regions above the temples; and the raven-black, the glossy, the luxuriant, the naturally curling tresses, setting forth the full force of the Homeric epithet, "hyacinthine." I looked at the delicate outline of the nose. . . .

But I refrain. It is easy enough to agree with Aldous Huxley and Yvor Winters, and dismiss this sort of ungrammatical rubbish as too vulgar, or even too idiotic, to reward the time it takes to point it out. But if Poe is worth understanding at all (I assume that he is), we might begin by asking why the writer of the lucid if not very distinguished passage from "William Wilson" repeatedly fell into the bathos of "Ligeia." I confess that Poe's serious style at its typical worst makes the reading of more than one story at a sitting an almost insuperable task. The Gothic glooms, the Venetian interiors, the ancient wine cellars (from which nobody ever enjoys a vintage but always drinks "deep")—all this, done up in a glutinous prose, so fatigues one's attention that with the best will in the world one gives up, unless one gets a clue to the power underlying the flummery.

I have tried in the course of these remarks to point in the direction in which the clue, as I see it, is to be found. I do not see it in the influence of the Gothic novel. This was no doubt there; but no man is going to use so much neo-Gothic, over and over again, unless he means business with it; I think that Poe meant business. If the Gothic influence had not been to hand, he would have invented it, or something equally "unreal" to serve his purpose. His purpose in laying on the thick décor was to simulate sensation. Poe's sensibility, for reasons that I cannot surmise here, was almost completely impoverished. He could feel little but the pressure of his predicament, and his perceptual powers remained undeveloped. Very rarely he gives us a real perception because he is not interested in anything that is alive. Everything in Poe is dead: the houses, the rooms, the furniture, to say nothing of nature and of human beings. He is like a child—all appetite without sensibility; but to be in manhood all appetite, all will, without sensibility, is to be a monster: to feed spiritually upon men without sharing with them a real world is spiritual vampirism. The description of Ligeia's head is that of a dead woman's.

Does it explain anything to say that this is necrophilism? I think not. Poe's prose style, as well as certain qualities of his verse,[2] ex-

---

[2] I expect to examine Poe's verse on another occasion. It may be remarked that his verse rhythms are for the metronome, not the human ear. Its real defects are so great that it is not necessary to invent others, as Mr. T. S. Eliot seems to do in *From Poe to Valéry* (New York, 1949). Thus Mr. Eliot (and I cite

presses the kind of "reality" to which he had access: I believe I have indicated that it is a reality sufficiently terrible. In spite of an early classical education and a Christian upbringing, he wrote as if the experience of these traditions had been lost: he was well ahead of his time. He could not relate his special reality to a wider context of insights—a discipline that might have disciplined his prose. From the literary point of view he combined the primitive and the decadent: primitive, because he had neither history nor the historical sense; decadent, because he was the conscious artist of an intensity which lacked moral perspective.

But writers tend to be what they are; I know of no way to make one kind into another. It may have been a condition of Poe's genius that his ignorance should have been what it was. If we read him as formal critics we shall be ready to see that it was another condition of his genius that he should never produce a poem or a story without blemishes, or a critical essay that, despite its acuteness in detail, does not evince provincialism of judgment and lack of knowledge. We must bear in mind Mr. Eliot's remark that Poe must be viewed as a whole. Even the fiction and the literary journalism that seem without value add to his massive impact upon the reader.

What that impact is today upon other readers I cannot pretend to know. It has been my limited task to set forth here a little of what one reader finds in him, and to acknowledge in his works the presence of an incentive (again, for one man) to self-knowledge. I do not hesitate to say that had Poe not written *Eureka,* I should have been able, a man of this age, myself to formulate a proposition of "inevitable annihilation." I can only invite others to a similar confession. Back of the preceding remarks lies an ambitious assumption, about the period in which we live, which I shall not make explicit. It is enough to say that, if the trappings of Poe's nightmare strike us as tawdry, we had better look to our own. That particular vision in its purity (Poe was very pure) is perhaps not capable of anything better than Mr. Poe's ludicrous décor. Nor

---

only one of his observations that seem to me wrong) complains that "the saintly days of yore" could not be an appropriate time for the Raven to have lived. Elijah was fed by Ravens, a bird which was almost extinct in America in the 1840's. Ravens frequently fed hermits and saints and were in fact a fairly standard feature of saintly equipment.

have persons eating one another up and calling it spiritual love often achieved a distinguished style either in doing it or in writing about it. It was not Ugolino, it was Dante who wrote about Ugolino with more knowledge than Ugolino had. Mr. Poe tells us in one of his simple poems that from boyhood he had "a demon in my view." Nobody then—my great-grandfather, my mother, three generations—believed him. It is time we did. I confess that his voice is so near that I recoil a little, lest he, Montressor, lead me into the cellar, address me as Fortunato, and wall me up alive. I should join his melancholy troupe of the undead, whose voices are surely as low and harsh as the grating teeth of storks. He is so close to me that I am sometimes tempted to enter the mists of pre-American genealogy to find out whether he may not actually be my cousin.

The Interpretation of "Ligeia"

by Roy P. Basler

Although a number of biographers, psychoanalytical and otherwise, have employed the data and theories of several schools of thought in nonrational psychology in attempting to interpret the personality of Poe, and have indicated the need for such an approach in the interpretation of much of his writing, no one, as far as I am aware, has undertaken to point out the specific bearing of nonrational psychology on the critical interpretation of a number of Poe's stories which in their entire context seem to indicate that Poe dealt deliberately with the psychological themes of obsession and madness. Such a story is "Ligeia," the most important of a group of stories, generally but inadequately classified as "impressionistic," which includes the kindred pieces "Morella" and "Berenice." Each of these three tales shows a similar preoccupation with the *idée fixe* or obsession in an extreme form of monomania which seems intended by Poe to be the psychological key to its plot. Even a casual comparison of these stories will reveal not merely the similar theme of obsession but also the dominant concepts which provide the motivation in all three: the power of the psychical over the physical and the power of frustrate love to create an erotic symbolism and mythology in compensation for sensual disappointment. Although Poe grinds them differently in each story, they are the same grist to his mill.

In the interpretation of "Ligeia" particularly, an understanding of the nonrational makes necessary an almost complete reversal of certain critical opinions and explanations which assume that the story is a tale of the supernatural. Clayton Hamilton's analysis of

"Ligeia" in his *Manual of the Art of Fiction* (1918) is a rationalization which outdoes Poe's rationalization of "The Raven" in its
attempt to show how Poe chose with mathematical accuracy just
the effect and just the word which would make the perfect story of
the supernatural. Unfortunately, Hamilton's basic assumptions seem
obviously erroneous when he takes for granted that Ligeia is the
main character, that the action of the story is concerned primarily
with her struggle to overcome death, that the hero (the narrator)
is "an ordinary character" who functions merely as an "eyewitness"
and as a "standard by which the unusual capabilities of the central
figure may be measured," and that Ligeia is "a woman of super-
human will, and her husband, a man of ordinary powers." These
assumptions ignore the obvious context with its emphasis on the
hero's obsession, madness, and hallucination. Actually, the story
seems both aesthetically and psychologically more intelligible as a
tale, not of supernatural, but rather of entirely natural, though
highly phrenetic, psychological phenomena.

Perhaps the naïveté and excesses of certain psychoanalytical biographies of Poe have militated against the recognition of the value
of nonrational psychology in the study of Poe. At any rate, scholarly
critical biographers have hesitated to credit the indubitable data
of the science; and even recent critical studies following the traditional interpretation, ignore the most obvious evidence of the nonrational theme and motivation of "Ligeia" and undertake to analyze
the story again as a tale of the supernatural. Although we need not
consider here either the value of nonrational psychology as a means
of understanding Poe's personality or the mistakes of broad assumption and overconfidence which the analysts of Poe have made, it
must be recognized that, if nonrational psychology provides a better
means of understanding the structure and effect of a tale like
"Ligeia" and enables the reader to appreciate better what Poe
accomplished as an artist, then the critic who refuses to accept nonrational psychology does so at the risk of his entire critical principle.

Let us examine the personality of the hero of "Ligeia," the
narrator whose psycho-emotional experience weaves the plot. He
is presented in the first paragraph as a man with an erotic obsession
of long standing; his wife is presumably dead, but his idolatrous
devotion to her has kept her physical beauty and her personality
painfully alive in his every thought. That this devotion approaches

monomania becomes more clear with every statement he makes about her. She is the acme of womanly beauty and spiritual perfection. From the time of his first acquaintance with her he has been oblivious of all but her beauty and her power over him: "I cannot, for my soul, remember how, when, or even precisely where, I first became acquainted with the lady Ligeia." Furthermore, there is his interesting admission that "I have *never known* the paternal name of her who was my friend and my betrothed, and who became the partner of my studies, and finally the wife of my bosom." In view of the fact that she was of an exceedingly ancient family and had brought him wealth "very far more, than ordinarily falls to the lot of mortals," these admissions are more than strange. Though the hero half recognizes the incongruity of his unbelievable ignorance, he dismisses it as evidence of a lover's devotion—a "wildly romantic offering on the shrine of the most passionate devotion."

Beginning with the second paragraph, we see more clearly the degree of his obsession. Although he makes much of the power of Ligeia's intellect, his imaginative preoccupation with her physical beauty is highly sensuous, even voluptuous, in its intensity. He seems to be a psychopath who has failed to find the last, final meaning of life in the coils of Ligeia's raven hair, her ivory skin, her "jetty lashes of great length," and, above all, in her eyes, "those shining, those divine orbs!" But his imaginative desire has outrun his capabilities. Though his senses have never revealed the final meaning of the mystery which has enthralled him, his imagination refuses to accept defeat. The key to his failure is hinted in the paragraph which reveals his symbolic deification of Ligeia as a sort of personal Venus Aphrodite who personifies the dynamic urge of life itself but who, because of the hero's psychic incapacity, cannot reveal to him the "forbidden knowledge";

> There is no point, among the many incomprehensible anomalies of the science of mind, more thrillingly exciting than the fact—never, I believe, noticed in the schools—that in our endeavors to recall to memory something long forgotten, we often find ourselves *upon the very verge* of remembrance, without being able, in the end, to remember. And thus how frequently, in my intense scrutiny of Ligeia's eyes, have I felt approaching the full knowledge of their expression—felt it approaching—yet not quite be mine—and so at length entirely depart! And (strange, oh, strangest mystery of all!)

I found, in the commonest objects of the universe, a circle of analogies to that expression. I mean to say that, subsequently to the period when Ligeia's beauty passed into my spirit, there dwelling as in a shrine, I derived, from many existences in the material world, a sentiment such as I felt always aroused within me by her large and luminous orbs. Yet not the more could I define that sentiment, or analyze or even steadily view it. I recognized it, let me repeat, sometimes in the survey of a rapidly-growing vine—in the contemplation of a moth, a butterfly, a chrysalis, a stream of running water. I have felt it in the ocean; in the falling of a meteor. I have felt it in the glances of unusually aged people. And there are one or two stars in heaven (one especially, a star of the sixth magnitude, double and changeable, to be found near the large star in Lyra) in a telescopic scrutiny of which I have been made aware of the feeling. I have been filled with it by certain sounds from stringed instruments, and not unfrequently by passages from books. Among innumerable other instances, I well remember something in a volume of Joseph Glanville, which (perhaps merely from its quaintness—who shall say?) never failed to inspire me with the sentiment;—"And the will therein lieth, which dieth not. Who knoweth the mysteries of the will, with its vigor? For God is but a great will pervading all things by nature of its intentness. Man doth not yield him to the angels, nor unto death utterly, save only through the weakness of his feeble will."

In this passage it is not difficult to perceive the oblique confession of inadequacy and to trace the psychological process of symbolism, which compensates for the failure of sense by apotheosis of the object of desire. Although sensuous delight leads the hero to "the very verge" of a "wisdom too divinely precious not to be forbidden," final knowledge of the secret of Ligeia's eyes is blocked by an obstacle deep within the hero's own psyche, and the insatiable imagination seeks for a realm of experience not sensual and mortal and identifies Ligeia with the dynamic power and mystery of the entire universe. She becomes not merely a woman but a goddess, through the worship of whom he "feels" that he may "pass onward to the goal of a wisdom too divinely precious not to be forbidden." There is for him, however, no possibility of fathoming the mystery which she symbolizes, though in the height of passionate adoration he feels himself to be *"upon the very verge,"* which experience he likens to that of almost but not quite recalling something from the depths of his unconscious.

This analogy of the will's inability to dictate to the unconscious and its inability to dictate to love reveals something more than the hero's vague awareness of a psychic flaw which thwarts his desire; it reveals the source of the obsession which dominates in a compensatory process his struggle to achieve by power of mind what he cannot achieve through love. The passage from Glanvill is the key, the psychic formula, which he hopes may open to him the very mystery of being, his own as well as Ligeia's, in which as he conceives lies the source of the dark failure and frustration of his senses. From this psychic formula derives, then, the megalomania that he can by power of will become godlike, blending his spirit with the universal spirit of deity symbolized in the divine Ligeia, who possesses in apotheosis all the attributes of his own wish, extended in a symbolic ideal beyond the touch of mortality and raised to the absoluteness of deity—intensity in thought, passion, and sensibility; perfection in wisdom, beauty, and power of mind. It is worth noting that Poe had earlier used the name Ligeia in *Al Aaraaf* for a divinity representing much the same dynamic beauty in all nature.

But the hero's approach to power is thwarted by Ligeia's death. Just at the point when triumph seems imminent, when he feels "that delicious vista by slow degrees expanding before me, down whose long, gorgeous, and all untrodden path, I might at length pass onward to the goal of a wisdom too divinely precious not to be forbidden"—just then Ligeia dies, because of the weakness of her own mortal will and in spite of the fervor with which the hero himself "struggled desperately in spirit with the grim Azrael."

At this point it may be noted that the obsession with the *idée fixe* expressed in the passage from Glanvill begins with the hero himself and does not express Ligeia's belief. It is his will to conquer death that motivates the rest of the story, not hers. Even when she recites the formula on her deathbed, the lines are but the echo of his wish, given in antiphonal response to the materialistic creed which she has avowed in her poem "The Conqueror Worm," which represents her philosophy and is read by the hero merely at her peremptory request. This fact is always overlooked in the rational interpretations of the story, which assume that Ligeia's struggle is the primary motivating action of the tale. Thus, in spite of her power and beauty and her passionate desire for life, *"but* for life," the earthly body of Ligeia dies—perhaps, as the obsessed hero conceives, because she has not believed in her power to conquer death. Her failure of spirit, however, is not the end. Nor is the hero's failure as he "struggled desperately in spirit with the grim Azrael" the end, but rather the beginning of the grim mania in which he is resolved to bring her back to life.

In following all that the hero says, the reader must keep constantly in mind that, if the hero is suffering from obsession, his narrative cannot be accepted merely at its face value as authentic of all the facts; and he must remember that incidents and circumstances have a primary significance in terms of the hero's mania which is often at variance with the significance which the hero believes and means to convey. This is to say that Poe's psychological effect in "Ligeia" is similar to that of later delvers in psychological complexity like Henry James, whose stories told by a narrator move on two planes. There is the story which the narrator means to tell, and there is the story which he tells without meaning to, as he unconsciously reveals himself.

Hence, the important elements in the hero's description of Ligeia are of primary significance as they reveal his feeling of psychic inadequacy, his voluptuous imagination, and his megalomania and fierce obsession with the idea that by power of will man may thwart death through spiritual love. Likewise, the narrative of the circumstances of Ligeia's death is of significance, not merely as it reveals her love of life and her struggle to live, but as it reveals the psychological crisis in which the hero's psychic shock and frustration bring on final and complete mania, the diagnostic fallacy of which is that his will is omnipotent and can bring Ligeia back to life. Up to the point of her death the hero's obsession has taken the form of adoration and worship of her person in an erotomania primarily sensual (though frustrated by a psychic flaw which he is aware of but does not understand) and hence projected into a symbolic realm of deity and forbidden wisdom. Following her death, however, his obsession becomes an intense megalomania motivated by his will to restore her to life in another body through a process of metempsychosis.

It is of particular importance that, with the beginning of the second half of the story, the reader keep in mind these two planes of meaning, for the primary significance of what the hero tells in this part is never in any circumstance the plain truth. It is rather an entirely, and obviously, fantastic representation of the facts, which justifies his obsessed psyche and proves that he has been right and Ligeia (and perhaps the gentle reader) wrong in the assumption that mortality is the common human fate—the old story of the madman who knows that he is right and the rest of the world wrong.

Thus even the hero's admission of his "incipient madness" must be recognized as the cunning condescension of the megalomaniac to the normal mind, which would not otherwise understand the excesses of his peculiar "childlike perversity" in choosing such macabre furnishings for his bridal chamber or in debauching his senses with opium—both of which "perversities" he dismisses with pseudo-naïveté as minor "absurdities." The contempt which he feels for people of normal mentality almost leads him to give himself away in his blistering question: "Where were the souls of the haughty family of the bride, when, through thirst of gold, they permitted to pass the threshold of an apartment *so* bedecked, a maiden and a daughter so beloved?" In other words, why could not the parents of Rowena perceive in the macabre furnishings—the "ebony couch" with draperies of gold "spotted all over, at regular intervals, with arabesque figures . . . of the most jetty black," the "sarcophagus of black granite," and the "endless succession of the ghastly forms which belong to the superstition of the Norman, or arise in the guilty slumbers of the monk"—why could they not perceive the obvious death chamber which he intended the bridal room to be? Likewise, one must recognize the maniacal condescension which prompts the hardly disarming naïveté with which he confesses the pleasure he derived from Rowena's dread avoidance of him in the "unhallowed hours of the first month of our marriage" and with which he testifies, "I loathed her with a hatred belonging more to demon than to man."

Perhaps he relies on this impercipiency of the normal mind to befuddle also the moral equilibrium of his audience into a sentimental acceptance of the phrenetic devotion of his spirit to the memory of Ligeia, which in his madness justifies, of course, his ghastly treatment of Rowena in terms of a pure, ethereal love for

Ligeia. Thus he concludes his introductory statement in the second half of the story on a plane which, while utterly sincere in its obsessional idealism, is highly equivocal in its moral and psychological implications and reveals the fact that underlying his mad persecution of Rowena lies his frustrate desire for and worship of the lost Ligeia:

> . . . My memory flew back (oh, with what intensity of regret!) to Ligeia, the beloved, the august, the beautiful, the entombed. I revelled in recollections of her purity, of her wisdom, of her lofty—her ethereal nature, of her passionate, her idolatrous love. Now, then, did my spirit fully and freely burn with more than all the fires of her own. In the excitement of my opium dreams (for I was habitually fettered in the shackles of the drug), I would call aloud upon her name, during the silence of the night, or among the sheltered recesses of the glens by day, as if, through the wild eagerness, the solemn passion, the consuming ardor of my longing for the departed, I could restore her to the pathways she had abandoned—ah, *could* it be forever?—upon the earth.

Up to this point in the second half of the story, the hero has unintentionally mixed a generous amount of obliquely truthful interpretation with the facts of his story; but from this point to the end he narrates events with a pseudo-objectivity that wholly, though not necessarily intentionally, falsifies their significance. He tells what he saw and heard and felt, but these things must be understood as the hallucinations of his mania, as wish-projections which arise from his obsession with the idea of resurrecting Ligeia in the body of Rowena. He tells the effects but ignores or misrepresents the causes: he wants his audience to believe that the power of Ligeia's will effected her resurrection in the body of Rowena but does not want his audience to recognize (what he himself would not) that he was the actual agent of Rowena's death and his perceptions mere hallucinations produced by obsessional desire.

In brief, it must be recognized that the hero has murdered Rowena in his maniacal attempt to restore Ligeia to life. Although his narrative of the "sudden illness" which seized Rowena "about the second month of the marriage" avoids anything which suggests a physical attempt at murder, there are unintentional confessions of deliberate psychological cruelty in the macabre furnishings of the apartment and in the weird sounds and movements designed to produce ghostly effects. The hero mentions with apparent casualness and objectivity that, "in her perturbed state of half-slumber, she spoke of sounds, and of motions, in and about the chamber of the turret, which I concluded had no origin save in the distemper of her fancy, or perhaps in the phantasmagoric influences of the chamber itself." But by his earlier confession he had calculated these "sounds" and "motions" in advance, as instruments of mental torture for the young bride, by so arranging the figured draperies as to produce optical illusions of motion and by introducing "a strong current of wind behind the draperies." He further confesses that as her dread and fear began to produce symptoms of hysteria and physical collapse he "wished to show her (what, let me confess it, I could not *all* believe) that those almost inarticulate breathings, and those very gentle variations of the figures upon the wall, were but the natural effects of that customary rushing of the wind." But he did not tell her!

At this point he narrates how he became aware of a "presence" in the chamber, a supernatural agency at work. This is the wish-illusion that not he but the ghost of Ligeia, vampire-like, is preying upon the distraught and febrile body of Rowena. The details of resuscitation and relapse he wishes to believe evidence of the struggle of Ligeia's spirit to drive Rowena's spirit out of the body and to reanimate it herself. Hence arises the hallucination of the shadow on the carpet—"a faint, indefinite shadow of angelic aspect—such as might be fancied for the shadow of a shade." But, as he admits immediately, he had indulged in "an immoderate dose of opium, and heeded these things but little, nor spoke of them to Rowena." Such deprecation of his own perception is again the cunning of the maniac who must tell his story and must equally not tell it wholly, lest he spoil it by supplying evidence of a sort likely to encourage suspicion that there is something more than opiumism in his madness.

Then comes the crux of the death scene. Here, in the mélange of fact and hallucination, is *the fact* which betrays him: "I saw, or may have dreamed that I saw, fall within the goblet, as if from some invisible spring in the atmosphere of the room, three or four large drops of a brilliant and ruby colored fluid." Impatient for results and fearful that the apparent progress of Rowena's hysteria and physical collapse will not suffice, doubting the power of his will alone to effect his purpose, he has resorted to actual poison, which, however, his obsession adapts into the pattern of hallucination by perceiving that it is distilled from the atmosphere rather than dropped from a bottle held in his own hand. He cannot in his obsession recognize the bottle or the poison as physical facts, for then the power of the spirit must bow to the greater power of a merely physical drug.

The deed is accomplished, and the remainder of the narrative reveals the final stage of his mania. As the body of Rowena writhes in the throes of death, his wish takes complete command of his brain. As he watches, his mind is filled with "a thousand memories of Ligeia." The shadow on the carpet disappears, and he hears "a sob, low, gentle, but very distinct," which he "*felt . . .* came from the bed of ebony." As evidence of returning life appears in the corpse, he feels it necessary that "some immediate exertion be made; yet the turret was altogether apart from the portion of the abbey tenanted by the servants—there were none within call—I had no means of summoning them to my aid without leaving the room for many minutes—and this I could not venture to do." With this obviously satisfactory explanation made, he relates how he struggled alone to call back "the spirit still hovering," only to fall back with a shudder and resume his "passionate waking visions of Ligeia."

Again and again the symptoms of life appear and diminish, and each time the hero testifies that he "sunk into visions of Ligeia," with the result that each period of struggle "was succeeded by I know not what of wild change in the personal appearance of the corpse," until finally his obsessed brain and senses perceive their desire-wish accomplished. The phrenetic tension of hallucination mounts in the concluding paragraph to an orgasm of psychopathic horror and wish-fulfilment in the final sentence: " 'Here, then, at least,' I shrieked aloud, 'can I never—can I never be mistaken—these are the full, and the black, and the wild eyes—of my lost love—of the Lady—of the Lady Ligeia!' "

This conclusion is artistically perfect and unassailable if the story is understood to be that of a megalomaniac, a revelation of obsessional psychology and mania. If, however, the story is taken to be a rational narrative of the quasi-supernatural told by a man in his right mind, the conclusion is not a conclusion but a climax, the proper denouement of which would be the corpse's reassumption of

Rowena's lineaments and its final lapse into certain death, recognized this time as complete and final by the mind of the hero. Philip Pendleton Cooke, presuming the entirely rational interpretation to be the one Poe intended, called Poe's attention to this supposed weakness of the ending in a letter otherwise filled with large praise for the story's effect. Cooke's comment is as follows:

> There I was shocked by a violation of the ghostly proprieties—so to speak—and wondered how the Lady Ligeia—a wandering essence—could, in quickening *the body of the Lady Rowena* (such is the idea) become suddenly the visible, bodily Ligeia.

Poe's answer takes full cognizance of the justice of Cooke's criticism and tacitly admits the rational interpretation to be the one he intended, making the somewhat lame excuse that

> . . . it was necessary, since "Morella" was written, to modify "Ligeia." I was forced to be content with a sudden half-consciousness, on the part of the narrator, that Ligeia stood before him. One point I have not fully carried out—I should have intimated that the *will* did not perfect its intention—there should have been a relapse—a final one—and Ligeia (who had only succeeded in so much as to convey an idea of the truth to the narrator) should be at length entombed as Rowena—the bodily alterations having gradually faded away.

It is possible that Poe meant in this statement merely to bow to Cooke's praise and accept a criticism which completely misses the primary significance of the entire story, in order to avoid the necessity of explaining to an admirer the painful truth that he had missed the point. Poe was avid for the praise that came all too seldom, and he may have avoided controversy with his appreciative correspondent somewhat out of gratitude. That he could not have held seriously or for long the opinion that the story needed an added denouement seems obvious from the fact that, although he made careful and detailed revisions of the story afterward, he did not alter the nature of the conclusion. That he would have done so without hesitation had he actually believed the conclusion defective, we may be sure from his indefatigable practice of revising his favorite pieces even in the minor details which did not fulfil his wishes.

There seem to be two alternatives here: either Poe meant the story to be read as Cooke read it, and failed to provide the sort of conclusion which he admitted to be necessary, or he meant it to be read approximately as we have analyzed it, and merely bowed to Cooke's criticism out of gratitude for appreciation. Possibly there is a third alternative, however, which is not incompatible with Poe's genius. Perhaps the intention in the story was not entirely clear and rationalized in Poe's own mind, preoccupied as he was with the very ideas and obsessions which motivate the hero of the story. Anyone who has studied Poe's rationalization of "The Raven" in "The Philosophy of Composition" must recognize that in its *post hoc* reasoning Poe largely ignores the obvious psycho-emotional motivation of his own creative process. In his offhand and casual comments on his writings, however, he sometimes admitted the essentially "unconscious" source of his compositions. An example of this admission is his comment written in a copy of the *Broadway Journal* which he sent to Mrs. Sarah Helen Whitman:

> The poem ["To Helen"—of 1848] which I sent you contained all the events of a *dream* which occurred to me soon after I knew you. Ligeia was also suggested by *a dream*—observe the *eyes* in both tale and poem.

As an artist Poe depicted the functioning of both rational and nonrational processes in a character obsessed by a psychopathic desire. But, since Poe was not entirely clear in his own mind concerning the nonrational logic of the unconscious which he used as an artist, he accepted Cooke's criticism as justified, even though he felt the "truth" and appropriateness of the conclusion as he had written it, in part, at least, out of his own unconscious. Poe's penciled comment on the manuscript copy of one of his later poems, as quoted by Mrs. Whitman, is again indicative of the source of his artistic if not of his critical certainty:

> "All that I have here expressed was actually present to me. Remember the mental condition which gave rise to 'Ligeia'—recall the passage of which I spoke, and observe the coincidence . . . I regard these visions," he says, "even as they arise, with an awe which in some measure moderates or tranquillizes the ecstacy—I so regard them through a conviction that this ecstacy, in itself, is of a character supernal to the human nature—*is a glimpse of the spirit's outer world.*"

Thus, when he came to revise the story, his artistic sense, rooted deeply in his own unconscious processes (or, if one chooses, in "the spirit's outer world"), did not permit the alteration of the conclusion to fit an interpretation essentially superficial and incomplete in its perception of the psychological origin of the story. Had Poe been able to understand the nonrational processes of the psyche as fully as Freud did later, he might have written a reply to Cooke that would have outdone "The Philosophy of Composition" in logical analysis of the creation of a work of art out of both rational and nonrational mental processes, but it is not likely that he could have written as an artist a more effective psychological story than "Ligeia."

The merits of this analysis must, of course, stand or be dismissed on the evidence within the context of the story itself, and the evidence in this case is—what it is not in the case of Poe's personality —complete. The hero of the story either is or is not to be completely trusted as a rational narrator whose account can be accepted with the meaning which he wishes it to have, and Poe either does or does not give the reader to understand which point of view he must take. To me, at least, Poe makes obvious the fact of the hero's original obsession in the first half of the story and his megalomania in the second half. The concluding paragraph remains aesthetically as utterly incomprehensible to me as it was to Philip Pendleton Cooke, if the story is merely a story of the supernatural designed to produce an impression. And I cannot think that Poe, fully aware of the justice of Cooke's criticism in that view, would have left the denouement as it was originally written unless he believed that there was more artistic verisimilitude in the story as he had created it than there was in the story as Cooke had interpreted it.

The French Response to Poe

by Patrick F. Quinn

"Edgar Poe, who isn't much in America, *must* become a great man in France—at least that is what I want." [1] When Baudelaire wrote those words to Sainte-Beuve in 1856, he had already given nine years to a task that was to preoccupy him for seven years more. It was only when a paralytic stroke shattered him in 1866 that Baudelaire abandoned, along with all lesser interests, this one which had dominated most of his mature life. One of the results of this remarkable devotion is that of the twelve volumes of Baudelaire's works in the definitive Crépet edition, five are translations from the work of Poe. This simple arithmetic involves a fact of major significance. For in Baudelaire there was a great creative genius, a writer who had, and knew he had, one of the rarest of all gifts: the power to alter and revivify his own country's literature. And yet this man, for nearly twenty years, gave himself with an almost ascetic energy and ardor to the wearisome and specifically uncreative work of sedulous translating. Certainly this was no pastime for him, nor was it simply the means of obtaining an income, although it did serve that end, too. One is almost tempted to go so far as to say that Baudelaire's life work, his great achievement, was not so much *Les Fleurs du mal* as it was his Poe translations. However this may be, the five Poe volumes fulfilled and surpassed all that Baudelaire had hoped for them. Not only did Poe become a great man in France; he has become, thanks to Baudelaire, a world figure, and this despite

   [1] Baudelaire, *Correspondance*, I, 380. Unless otherwise indicated, all references to the writings of Baudelaire, his correspondence and his Poe translations, pertain to *Œuvres complètes de Charles Baudelaire,* ed. Jacques Crépet (Paris, 1923-1953), 19 vols.

the fact that his reputation as a major writer in America has hardly been better than precarious. Let us examine this astonishing paradox.

Although it is a commonplace that in American literature there are few writers of really major rank, it is perilous to offer an opinion as to just who these writers are. Whatever the list, the objection will be made that the prizes were not fairly awarded. But it seems fairly certain that if the list is a brief one Poe's claims for inclusion in it are by no means considered self-evident in this country, and have seldom been convincingly sponsored. The general reading public, which might be expected to show a warm interest in Poe, or at least a dutiful respect for him, has shown neither. Some forty years after his death, when a poll was taken to discover which ten books were generally considered the best to be written in America, Emerson's *Essays* and Hawthorne's *Scarlet Letter* reached the top of the list. Nothing by Poe was voted to rank among the first ten, or the first thirty! [2] No doubt Poe would fare better today if a similar competition were arranged, but it seems true nonetheless that his status as a classic American author exists, in the mind of the general public, rather by default than acclaim.

If apathy will serve to characterize the attitude of the common reader towards Poe, something more like hostility has been the usual response of American writers from Poe's time to our own. Emerson, for example, employed his considerable talents as a phrasemaker to dispose of him in three words, "the jingle man." [3] Whitman's feelings were mixed: although he finally came round to admitting Poe's genius, it was its narrow range and unhealthy, lurid quality that most impressed him. But Whitman did manage to attend the Poe Memorial ceremony in Baltimore in 1875, and although he declined to speak publicly there, he at least had the charity to lend his distinguished presence to that pathetic occasion.[4] This was more than the other leading American poets of the day could bring themselves to do. From Bryant, Whittier, Longfellow, and Holmes came brief and "appropriate" tributes, none of which

[2] D. R. Hutcherson, "Poe's Reputation in England and America, 1850-1909," *American Literature*, XIV (November, 1942), 223.

[3] As reported by William Dean Howells in *Literary Friends and Acquaintances* (New York & London, 1901), pp. 60-64.

[4] Whitman describes this occasion and sums up his impressions of Poe in *Specimen Days* (*Prose Works*, Camden edition, I, 284-87).

approached the intensity of feeling and conviction expressed in the letter Swinburne sent from England. And to compare the perfunctory doggerel offered by Bryant as a tombstone inscription with the incandescent sonnet Mallarmé had submitted is to realize, quite apart from the abyss that separates verse from poetry, in which hemisphere Poe's work had been really welcomed. Only recently, in some essays by T. S. Eliot and Allen Tate, has American criticism begun to treat Poe in a way that suggests an awareness of the implications of that sonnet.[5] From Henry James ("An enthusiasm for Poe is the mark of a decidedly primitive stage of reflection") through Paul Elmer More ("Poe is the poet of unripe boys and unsound men") to Yvor Winters ("Poe . . . whose literary merit appears to the present writer a very frail delusion"),[6] our critics, far from pushing Poe onto the stage of world literature, have rather insisted that his name be retained exclusively as a minor one even in the cast of American letters.

How different a chart must be plotted to show the history of Poe's reputation in France! His American contemporaries were reluctant to pay him merely conventional homage; for his French admirers the problem was to find a language of praise sufficiently sublime. Baudelaire, of course, carried away by his missionary zeal, was not one to hesitate on this subject. In *L'Art romantique* he calls Poe simply "the most powerful writer of the age." [7] Make what allowances we will for this as a statement intended for public consumption, the sincerity underlying it may be inferred from the allusion, in *Journaux intimes,* to his morning prayers to God and

[5] Eliot's essay on Poe appeared originally in a French translation by Henri Fluchère in *La Table ronde,* No. 12 (December 1948), pp. 1973-92. The English text, curiously different in a few details from the French version, was published (not for sale) by Harcourt, Brace in New York in 1948, and was printed in *The Hudson Review,* II (Autumn 1949), 327-42. Allen Tate's essays may be found in *The Forlorn Demon* (Chicago, 1953). In 1926, it was Edmund Wilson's opinion that "no recent American critic, with the exception of Mr. Waldo Frank in his article on the Poe-Allan letters, has written with any real appreciation of Poe's absolute artistic importance." The situation has not greatly improved, despite Wilson's own fine essay "Poe at Home and Abroad," from which this opinion is quoted. See *The Shores of Light* (New York, 1952), pp. 179-90.

[6] See James's essay on Baudelaire in *French Poets and Novelists* (London, 1878), p. 76; P. E. More, "A Note on Poe's Method," *Studies in Philology,* XX (July 1923), 309; Yvor Winters, "Edgar Allan Poe: A Crisis in the History of American Obscurantism," in *Maule's Curse* (Norfolk, 1938), p. 304.

[7] *L'Art romantique,* p. 59.

to Edgar Poe as his intercessor in heaven.[8] For Mallarmé also, Poe was a writer altogether unique, *the* poet, as we know from "Le Tombeau d'Edgar Poe." For him as for Baudelaire the stature of Poe was evidently that of a literary deity. Thus when Mallarmé sent to his friend Cazalis a copy of his sonnet "L'Azur," the first in which he had completely succeeded in the style that was to be distinctively his own, he remarked in his letter: "The more I continue in this direction the more faithful shall I be to those severe ideas which I owe to my great master Edgar Poe." [9] And for Valéry in the next generation Poe was also to be a great master: "Poe is the only impeccable writer. He was never mistaken." [10] In the first letter he wrote to Mallarmé, in 1890, Valéry was careful to underline their common admiration of Poe; and fifty years later he was to specify Poe, along with Leonardo Da Vinci, as the major influences in his literary and philosophical career.[11]

That an enthusiasm for Poe should have been shared by the three most influential poets in modern French literature, that this American writer should have become the pivot on which for the past century French literature has turned, this by itself is sufficiently extraordinary. But even this statement of the case does no more than suggest the force of Poe's impact. There is scarcely one French writer from the time of Baudelaire to the present who has not in one way or another paid his respects to Poe. Villiers de l'Isle Adam, Verlaine and Rimbaud, Huysmans, Claudel, Gide, Edmond Jaloux —these are names at random, but they will serve to indicate the scope of the interest Poe has had for France. Indeed the only *short* list of French writers that would be relevant to this subject would consist of those men, like Barbey d'Aurevilly and Sainte-Beuve, who did not join the pilgrimage to the Poe shrine. For this interest became something very like a religious cult. If Baudelaire was unique in actually praying to Edgar Poe, some of Baudelaire's successors were not far behind him in their fervent devotion. For the adherents to this cult Poe becomes immense, transcendent, to be associated, as he is by Jules Lemaître, only with the very greatest figures,

---

[8] *Journaux intimes*, ed. Crépet (Paris, 1938), p. 49.

[9] Henri Mondor, *Vie de Mallarmé* (Paris, 1941), p. 104.

[10] Letter to Gide in 1891, quoted in Berne-Joffroy, *Présence de Valéry* (Paris, 1944), p. 216.

[11] See Valéry's preface to René Fernandat, *Autour de Paul Valéry* (Paris & Grenoble, 1944), p. ii.

Plato and Shakespeare.[12] The Poe text, accordingly, is conned with the fanatic zeal appropriate to sacred books. Thus Jean Moréas, in an article in *Le Symboliste,* could assume that the readers of that journal would appreciate a reference to one of Poe's least known stories, "The Devil in the Belfry." [13] And what if not religious awe is this, registered by Albert Samain in his *Carnets intimes:*

> Have read Edgar Poe, *Eureka.* Overwhelming sensation, especially towards the end. The grandeur of the hypotheses, the limitless nature of the concept, terrify me. I wanted to read it through in one night, and this dizzy flight through the incommensurable makes me collapse on my bed, my body aching, my head splitting." [14]

No matter how the chart is read, therefore, whether we attend to such men as Baudelaire and Mallarmé or to writers of secondary and tertiary importance, the results are identical: Baudelaire made Poe a great figure in France, and not for his own time only but for the next hundred years. This apotheosis is probably unmatched in literature. Precisely because it is such an extraordinary thing, involving a great mass of subtleties and complications, it will perhaps never be definitively explained. But, to cut through the mass of detail for the moment, we can discern one unmistakable fact: the values France has attached to Poe are not those his own nation has seen in him. May it not be possible now to recapture Poe, as it were, for America, with at least some of those values still intact? It seems assured, to repeat a basic point, that if Poe is ever to be seriously appreciated in this country it will not be owing to traditional American criticism. It is rather to France that we must look; and in this chapter, in order to get a general impression of the central French thesis regarding Poe, we shall here survey three related instances of the French response to him, and then, in the next chapter, examine the whole phenomenon in greater detail.

I

In August 1845 a translation of "The Purloined Letter" appeared in a Paris journal, but neither Poe's name nor that of the

---

[12] Jules Lemaître, "Dialogue des morts," *Les Lettres et les arts* (January 1, 1886), pp. 139-44.

[13] *Le Symboliste* (October 7, 1886), p. 1.

[14] Albert Samain, *Carnets intimes* (Paris, 1939), p. 50.

translator was given. Later in that year a version of "The Gold Bug" was printed, this time with Poe named as the author. These were the beginnings of Poe's career in France.

Baudelaire did not become aware of this new writer immediately. He dated his discovery of him to some time in 1846, or 1847. But the strange commotion which he experienced in first reading Poe was a subject he never tired of alluding to. From the few French translations that were available he went on to what he could find in English. He wrote to London for a copy of Poe's works in book form; he collected a file of the *Southern Literary Messenger* during the period of Poe's editorship. And the more he investigated the matter the more his original feeling about Poe was confirmed. This American was his *alter ego,* his brother. "The first time I opened one of his books I saw, to my amazement and delight, not simply certain subjects which I had dreamed of, but *sentences* which I had thought out, written by him twenty years before." [15] This experience of the shock of recognition as Baudelaire describes it here is unparalleled in literature.

There is no reason to doubt that the experience was genuine. For one thing, Baudelaire recurs to it, in his letters and elsewhere, again and again, and always in the same terms and in the same tone. Any effort to dodge the implications of such evidence derives not from an expert understanding of Baudelaire but rather from a tacit assumption regarding Poe: that he is not really so impressive as Baudelaire thought he was. To examine Baudelaire's reaction to Poe with the premise in mind that he was not speaking in earnest is inevitably to befog the entire question. No such reservations are called for. The language Baudelaire uses to describe the effect Poe had on him is quite devoid of ambiguity.

There are other grounds also for not questioning the sincerity of his enthusiasm on this subject. Precisely because the experience was so profound, so unusual, Baudelaire was never able to examine Poe with any degree of critical detachment. Thus it is that after we have taken note of the extraordinary expression which Baudelaire gave to his interest in Poe and turn to the three long essays which he wrote on this subject, we feel, inevitably, rather let down. Nowhere in them does Baudelaire sustain his discussion on the level

[15] *Correspondance,* IV, 277.

which his brief remarks elsewhere have led us to think is the level
on which Poe should be treated. These essays, as examples of
criticism, are therefore disappointing. What Poe meant to Baudelaire as a kind of literary hero comes through clearly enough. But
what is said about the work of Poe seems rather superficial. It is as
if Baudelaire, no matter how intense his emotional response to this
work, could not readily communicate the secret of his feelings about
it. He could only make some suggestions; he could not coolly stand
apart and analyze. That so gifted a critic should have become
tongue-tied on the subject of his greatest enthusiasm is an indication
of how deeply implicated in Poe's work Baudelaire felt himself to
be. To probe into it, to discourse on its significance and the nature
of its life, would be, so it seems, to explore himself. This Baudelaire
was unwilling or unable to do. Hence his repeated requests to
Sainte-Beuve to write some critical articles on the subject of Poe.
"You, who so love profundities, why not investigate the profundities
of Edgar Poe?" [16] But Sainte-Beuve never fulfilled this request, or
any other which Baudelaire made regarding Poe. And so those
"profundities" which Baudelaire was sure existed in Poe's work, but
which he himself did not explore and could only point to, remained
unsounded for many years, until in our own time Baudelaire's
invitation to Sainte-Beuve was accepted by other writers.

There is some irony in the fact that the very feature which makes
Baudelaire's essays on Poe disappointing is their similarity to the
kind of essays Sainte-Beuve himself wrote.[17] From our contemporary
point of view, the attention given to the man and the milieu is
excessive. We would rather have, if we had the choice, much less of
that, and, instead, a much more detailed inquiry into what Poe
wrote. But despite their biographical emphasis, Baudelaire's essays

[16] *Correspondance,* II, 212.

[17] There is even greater irony in the fact, recently brought to light, that the
first of these essays, "Edgar Poe, sa vie et ses ouvrages," was not original with
Baudelaire! It has proved to be a translation of an article on Poe written by
John W. Daniel and published in the *Southern Literary Messenger* in 1850.
Baudelaire added some remarks of his own and some others which he found
in an obituary notice on Poe written by John R. Thompson for the November
1849 issue of the same magazine. See W. T. Bandy, "New Light on Baudelaire
and Poe," *Yale French Studies,* No. 10, pp. 65-69. In a forthcoming edition of
"Baudelaire's" first essay, Mr. Bandy will discuss the implications of this discovery. Meantime it may be said that this evidence does not help strengthen
the assumption that the Poe revered in Europe may be dismissed as a figment
of "the French imagination."

are not simply portraits of an artist who was exhausted and crushed in a materialistic, "counting-house" world. Naturally this interpretation of Poe's career would be favored, for Baudelaire saw in it all the more reason for his initial and intuitive feeling of kinship with Poe. Thus one clear purpose of the essays was to inscribe Poe's name in the roll of literary martyrs, along with the classic cases of Chatterton and Nerval. However, Baudelaire was not content with a merely sentimental view of the matter, one which would amount to saying that Poe's greatness was nothing more than an index of his weakness. Poe as a lame giant, then—this is what the portrait comes to. But a giant nonetheless, and this because of the complex interest which Poe's work contains. Baudelaire did not stop short with the presentation of a curious personality whose sad career furnished a lesson for the times. He called attention to a writer who should be taken seriously, and he indicated the channels down which this interest should move.

As Poe's translator, Baudelaire gave his attention almost entirely to the stories. But in his essays he had something suggestive to say of every aspect of Poe's work. "His poetry, profound and plaintive, is nevertheless wrought and pure, correct and brilliant as a crystal jewel." [18] Inspired? That too; but in addition the work of a man of will, master of himself, who realized that in art there can be no minutiae. Mallarmé was fascinated by hints such as these and took up a task which Baudelaire had thought impossible, the translating of Poe's poems. Poe's aesthetic, exacting and disciplined, calling for a union of inspiration and method [19]—this was to be the focus of Valéry's interest. Of Poe's *Eureka* Baudelaire had said that it would require an essay all to itself; in "A Propos d'Eureka" Valéry wrote that essay.

Baudelaire's successors thus found in the articles on Poe a number of hints which they acted on according to their own interests and predilections. For Baudelaire himself it was Poe's work in fiction that chiefly mattered, and it is not surprising that his most illuminating remarks are those he made on this subject. In general, he indicated that the stories were not to be read as mechanical melodramas, as contrived exercises in the horror genre. The "new

[18] "Edgar Poe, sa vie et ses œuvres," in *Histoires extraordinaires par Edgar Poe*, p. xxviii.
[19] "Notes nouvelles sur Edgar Poe," in *Nouvelles histoires extraordinaires par Edgar Poe*, p. xviii.

literature" which Poe had created would be devoid of all novelty if they were merely that. Consequently, Baudelaire took care to underscore the psychological content of these stories as their distinguishing feature. Much as he admired Poe's talent for ratiocination, and the "impeccable" quality of his style, the real Poe, for him, was "the writer of the nerves," who in exploring mental and moral disease had opened up for literature an order of experience that seemed to have been effectively sealed off. In his preface to *Tales of the Grotesque and Arabesque* (1840), Poe hinted that the terror he was writing about was "not of Germany but of the soul." In substance, this is what Baudelaire had to say about the spirit in which Poe's stories should be read.

Here again we find no more than a direction given. It was something, however, to make this point clearly, to define Poe's characteristic subject matter as belonging to the psychological order, and, if only by implication, to warn against the superficiality of seeing his work as the imitative productions of a sensational journalist who had some skill at writing weird tales. Baudelaire succeeded in setting up a strong barrier against such a misconception. It is chiefly as a result of this that subsequent French commentary on Poe has been so fecund. In this country, on the other hand, the prevailing view has been at best an uneasy one, unsure whether Poe's tales should not be dismissed as so much claptrap. In American criticism, ancient or modern, the treatment Poe has received has as a rule been either lean with censure or fat with platitude, and thus has generally failed to give a satisfactory account of his undeniable permanence and power.

II

Baudelaire pointed in a general way to the psychological interest of Poe's work, and this interest, as we shall see in more detail later, has been to the fore in France ever since. But the most striking demonstration of it is the two-volume study by Marie Bonaparte, *Edgar Poe,* published in Paris in 1933. It is one of the many ironies in the history of Poe's reputation that this, the most exhaustive scrutiny of his work, should have been written in French; that it should remain at this date so little known in this country (unmentioned, for example, in the bibliographical volume of *Literary*

History of the United States); and that the recent (1949) translation should have been published in England, but not here until 1954. In his review of this book Edmond Jaloux called it the most important critical study of Poe ever written in France.[20] And he added the interesting qualification that this holds true quite apart from the veracity of the particular psychological theory which Mme Bonaparte employs.

Thus he forestalled a common objection; for the theory employed is psychoanalysis, and when that word comes up in a literary context it is usually considered good form to knit one's brow and show signs of impatience. Often enough, perhaps, this stock response proves to be the right one. But in the realm of what is called literary psychoanalysis *Edgar Poe* is, I think, unique. No other study based on similar assumptions presents so elaborately detailed an examination of a writer and his work.[21] This is far from being the production of an amateur who, after leafing through a number of Freudian manuals, set out to develop a thesis on a likely author. Nor does it in any way resemble the rather cut and dried "depth" studies which some professional psychiatrists with a bookish turn have contributed to *The American Imago*. Once a friend and disciple of Freud, and today his most active and best known exponent in France, Marie Bonaparte does bring a rare professional competence to her task. But she brings also two other qualifications that are not often encountered in works of this kind, a wide erudition and a high degree of literary sensitivity. Thoroughly acquainted with English, she works with the standard "Virginia" edition of Poe, and, for the biographical section of her study, she follows the Hervey Allen volumes, the most authentic life of Poe that was available to her. Thus, whatever reservation is finally taken to the premises she starts from, no drastic demur may be raised against the scholarly foundations on which her work rests.

Her central thesis may be stated in this way: Poe's life and writings are fully intelligible only if it is assumed that they both derive their character from an infantile oedipal experience of great intensity. Love for his sickly, dying, and finally dead mother became

---

[20] *Nouvelles littéraires* (September 23, 1933), p. 3.
[21] Similar assumptions underline *Edgar Allan Poe: A Study in Genius*, by Joseph Wood Krutch. This book antedates the work of Marie Bonaparte by seven years. It is still worth reading, but in wealth of explicative detail her *Edgar Poe* is on an altogether different plane.

a kind of protean matrix which shaped the pattern of his life, and the recurrent themes of his tales, poems, and even *Eureka*. Poe was, in her description, "sado-necrophile." Such was his illness, and from that rank source arose the strange growths of his literary creation.

Yet to reduce *Edgar Poe* to an abstract statement of its theme is to distort it rather crudely. Nothing less will suffice for an understanding of the full complexities of the case than a careful reading of the entire work. Not that such a reading will dissipate all the difficulties that a study of this nature entails. It may be objected, for example, that psychoanalysis is, properly, nothing more than a therapy for living human beings; and therefore to read Poe's stories and poems, as Mme Bonaparte does, as if they essentially were transcripts of dreams, is to do violence to psychoanalysis as well as to Poe. Or one may suspect that the particular *kind* of Freudian explication used in this book is unduly primitive—too hard and fast, labored, Ptolemaic. And one needs no wide acquaintance with Freudian speculation to notice the technique which this writer employs whereby the distinction between fact and hypothesis is conveniently blurred so that the latter may be put to work as if it had all the strength of the former. Nevertheless, in spite of such objections as these, the impression that remains after reading her book is a formidable one. Once a few inherently unprovable assumptions are granted, *Edgar Poe* goes on to cast a powerful light on its subject. Poe himself, who so loved ingenious and astonishing solutions to complex puzzles, would have applauded this remarkable reading of his career and writings.

For although Marie Bonaparte is a psychoanalyst first of all, she is also a highly gifted reader. It is possible that her main intention was to "prove" psychoanalysis by a demonstration of its exegetical power. However, she could not have gone very far in that direction unless she had possessed the essential art in literary criticism, the art of reading well. Responding to Poe's work with a highly sensitive intelligence, she calls our attention to many details that are inescapably present in it, but which, prior to her study, have generally gone unnoticed. No other critic, for example, has said such illuminating things about "Loss of Breath," "The Man That Was Used Up," and the other baffling items of this kind which even Poe specialists prefer to leave alone. Or, to name a story that is universally famous, "The Murders in the Rue Morgue," how are the introductory and the main episodes of the story related? Why is the corpse of the murdered daughter discovered in the chimney head down? Why does the detective Dupin fail to explain that detail, or to inquire why the two murdered women should have been looking through a packet of letters at three in the morning? And how is this story related to "The Purloined Letter," where again a fireplace and a letter are important factors in the plot? Questions of this kind, which lead us directly to the author's text and on into a theory of what the text communicates, are raised and answered throughout her book. It is surprising enough that specific questions like these have not been raised before, but it is even more so to find how plausibly they may be answered in the light of Mme Bonaparte's guiding hypothesis. For that hypothesis, lurid as some of its results are, enables her to show an amazing homogeneity throughout the entirety of Poe's work. On any showing this is an impressive achievement.

III

Like almost all the discussions of Poe that have been written in France since the appearance of the Bonaparte volumes, those of Gaston Bachelard are indebted to her analysis. Bachelard's readings of Poe cannot be treated, however, as if they were merely an extension of her theories. They must be seen in the light of the rather special work he has been concerned with during the past twenty years, and on this intricate subject I shall attempt a word of explanation here.

For some years prior to his recent retirement at the age of seventy, Bachelard was professor of philosophy and head of the Institute of the History of Science and Techniques at the University of Paris. Encyclopedic in his interests, at home in physics, chemistry, and mathematics, and apparently as widely read in literature as any man in France, this extraordinary figure is above all a philosopher, creative, seminal, original. Original, and therefore iconoclastic. It was this bent that led him, in the course of his research into the work of the alchemists and pre-scientific "scientists" of the seventeenth and eighteenth centuries, to go beyond merely descriptive cataloging. Granted, he seems to have said, that these men were not really scientists and so gave us nothing that we recognize as scientific knowledge; yet neither were they merely stupid men. What, then, is the lesson their pre-scientific experience contains? In his analysis of this problem Bachelard developed the thesis that a psychology could be worked out for subjective knowledge, for intuition and reverie, the realm midway between dream and conscious thought. This is, precisely, the realm of the imagination. It was accordingly to the evidence of imaginative literature that he turned for the detailed demonstration of this theory. Resurrecting the ancient intuition that correspondences exist between the four elements and the human temperaments, Bachelard has presented in five volumes—from *La Psychanalyse du feu* (1938) to *La Terre et les rêveries du repos* (1948)—his amazing studies in the psychology of the imagination.

The rich suggestiveness of these books may be gauged from the fact that although relatively few pages deal with Poe those pages present some of the most illuminating commentary Poe has ever received. For Bachelard, Poe is, in general terms, a poet of water. That is the element towards which he was orientated and which polarized, so to speak, his imagination. This insight makes possible, among other things, a clear-cut demarcation between Poe and a writer with whom he is often associated, E. T. A. Hoffmann. A study of their imagery of water and fire shows how different they are: Hoffmann fascinated by flame, Poe recoiling compulsively from it, so that, as in "Ulalume," a volcano image is given in the form of "scoriac rivers," even though this fluvial effect weakens the figure Poe must have intended.[22] More specifically, Poe is the poet of darkened water, water which is stagnant, heavy, and dead. It absorbs life, drains it away. In a word, the water which fascinated Poe and which, in "Ulalume," "The City in the Sea," "Usher," and so on, is a dominant image, is no longer the "real" water which is drunk, but *that which drinks*. In an essay of thirty pages in *L'Eau et les rêves,* Bachelard examines the stories and poems of Poe, bringing into relief the great attraction the symbol of the dank tarn and the sullen, melancholy pool had for the imagination of this writer.

Another valuable reading of Poe which we owe to Gaston Bachelard is contained in the preface which he wrote in 1944 for a new French edition of *Arthur Gordon Pym.* This book, he tells us, is

[22] *La Psychanalyse du feu* (Paris, 1938), p. 181.

much more than what it is usually taken to be. It is, of course, a realistic narrative of adventures at sea; but at the same time it involves more than a merely social, human, conflict. It presents a drama of cosmic forces, a drama in which man is struggling against not simply human adversaries but the elements themselves. If the reader is to become aware of this drama he must bring to the book a special sympathy which grows out of the recognition that in Poe's best work there is both a manifest and a latent content. Beneath the surface account of more or less credible incident there is a subcurrent which flows from the world of dreams. Bachelard defines Poe's special quality in these terms. He admires Poe as one of the few writers who have been able to work along the frontier between the real and the dream worlds, a shadowy frontier where the writer's experience is strangely blended of elements drawn from both those realms.

Thus, in his comments on Poe, Bachelard accomplishes two important things. For one, he directs attention to the particular element-symbol in terms of which the Poe imagination was frequently aligned; and in addition he indicates and illustrates the technique of the double reading, through which alone, in his opinion, we can become aware of the kind of life that sustains Poe's melodramas. It is true, then, that although Bachelard treats Poe incidentally, as simply one exemplification of a recondite hypothesis, his discussion refines the exhaustive critique of Marie Bonaparte. Making a subtler use of some of the assumptions of psychoanalysis, less dogmatic and systematic in method, he nonetheless retains the essence of her theory (it was Baudelaire's as well): that Poe's singular gift was to probe into the caverns of the psyche and to bring up to the level of imaginative literature the dark scrolls—of fear, guilt, and obsession—that those caverns contain.

However true it is that the final and defining task in literary criticism is the task of evaluation, it is certainly true also that the initial work that must be done is to determine as exactly as possible *what is there*. With a writer like Poe this first step is indispensable, for it is a hallmark of Poe's work that it cannot easily be accounted for under any of the conventional headings. Baudelaire was aware of this when, with no success, he urged Sainte-Beuve to investigate the profundities of Edgar Poe. If now we have some conception of the extent of those profundities, some definable sense, in other words,

of what lies latent in Poe's work, it is in part because through their
development of this suggestion of Baudelaire the analyses of Marie
Bonaparte and Gaston Bachelard have given it to us, and indicated
at the same time what particular power it is that has insured Poe's
permanence among the great writers of the world.

Edgar Poe or The Theme of the Clock

by Jean-Paul Weber

It appears that the importance of the theme of the clock in Poe's work has not been adequately examined by critics. What gives rise to the present study is a double astonishment at the omnipresence of clocks in Poe's writings and at the absence of clocks in commentaries on his works. We shall begin with the most illuminating of Poe's texts.

"The Devil in the Belfry"

The epigraph of the tale ("What o'clock is it?") immediately suggests the realm of clocks and hours. Many an allusion, furthermore, underscores the same theme: the name of the borough where the action unfolds (Vondervotteimittiss, that is to say, *Wonder what time it is,* pronounced with a Dutch accent); the sundial which stands before each house in the village; the timepieces which the woodworkers of Vondervotteimittiss have carved everywhere; the clocks on the mantel pieces; the "little China man having a large stomach with a great round hole in it, through which is seen the dial-plate of a watch"; etc. One notices also the extraordinarily precise indications of time in the tale: "it wanted five minutes of noon"; "it wanted only three minutes of noon"; "just as it wanted half a minute of noon"; "it now wanted only half a second of noon." We may mention, finally, one of the "important resolutions" of the Town Council: "That we will stick to our clocks. . . ." One must bear in mind, moreover, the explicit plot of the story: thrown out of order by the imp, the clock in the belfry strikes thirteen at noon.

"Edgar Poe or The Theme of the Clock" by Jean-Paul Weber. From *La Nouvelle Revue Française*, 68 and 69 (August, September 1958), 301-11, 498-508. Translated by Claude Richard and Robert Regan. Reprinted by permission of the author.

But we must go further: even when the tale does not explicitly mention any element belonging to the realm of clocks, it harbors symbolic references to that realm.

Let us first consider the structure of the village "What Time Is It?" Oddly enough, it is circular. It is a "continuous row" of houses all standing "round the skirts" of a "perfectly circular" valley. At the periphery of the borough the "continuous row" consists of sixty houses. Inasmuch, then, as sixty houses stand in a circle at the outer limit of Vondervotteimittiss—sixty *identical* houses, set in regular order, all of them looking "to the center of the plain"—they stand for, they represent, the sixty minutes marked off on the circular periphery of a clock face.

In the light of this initial deciphering, we may easily comprehend some other characteristics of the borough: the valley, which the houses skirt, "is quite level and paved throughout with flat tiles" (the smooth and flat clock face); the houses have "their backs on the hills" (the marks which indicate minutes raised upon the clock face just inside the frame); the inhabitants "have never yet ventured to pass" these "gentle hills" (the "autarky" of the clock face, isolated from the exterior world; the immobility of the minute marks which "people" it).

And what of the two other major *hieroglyphs* of the story: the belfry and the devil?

The belfry rises "in the center" of the circular plain—that is to say of the clock face. Thus it must represent, it seems, one of the two hands when it has come close to the number "twelve." But which of the two? The hour hand or the minute hand? We have already emphasized that the sole explicit event in the story is the clock's striking noon. If we view the village as a clock face, and the event related by the tale regarding this clock face as the coming on of noon, it is obvious that the hand which rises vertically at the center of the clock face as noon approaches is the hour hand, that is to say, the smaller hand. Such would then be the sense of the belfry.

As for the devil, his meaning is transparent: he is the larger hand, the minute hand. His appearance as well as his actions give him away. His "tight-fitting swallow-tailed black coat" tends to give him an air of likeness with a clock hand, flared at the top, tapering toward the bottom. He moves "at a great rate"—like a minute hand as compared with the hour hand; at about twelve the devil comes to the belfry (the hour hand), makes himself at home, takes a seat. Thus at noon as at midnight, the minute hand coincides with the hour hand and covers it up ("There [the devil] sat in the belfry *upon the belfry-man, who was lying flat upon his back*"); the imp's settling in the belfry preludes the striking of the clock (just as the conjunction of the two hands at noon sets off the striking of twelve o'clock); and it follows the sounding of "the devil's tattoo" which the imp produces with a bass fiddle reminiscent of the tall cabinet of a standing clock (just as the striking of a grandfather clock is preceded by a creaking which issues from its "big" and "hollow" cabinet).

The symbols being so transparent, the implicit action of the tale must necessarily be, roughly speaking, closely akin to its manifest argument. The latter might be summed up thus: an imp, making an unforeseen appearance at the "belfry of the House of the Town-Council," throws the clock of that belfry out of order. The outline of the plot remains substantially unchanged when we view it in light of the preceding interpretation; the minute hand (the devil) meets the hour hand (the belfry) upon the circular clock face (the borough) and sets the bell striking thirteen, which shows that the mechanism is out of order. At the very most one could perceive in this little drama an unconscious desire to make a clock—a clock which remorselessly ticks away the minutes and chimes the hours—run excessively fast or slow.

It is relatively easy to understand the presence in Poe's unconscious of such a desire. In "William Wilson" a passage which scholars have recognized as manifestly autobiographical makes reference, apropos of Poe's "earliest recollections of a school-life," to two *clocks*. "At this moment," writes Poe, "I . . . thrill anew with undefinable delight, at the deep hollow note of the church-bell, breaking, each hour, with sullen and sudden roar, upon the stillness of the dusky atmosphere in which the fretted Gothic steeple lay imbedded and asleep."

Another clock ornaments Poe's schoolroom—a schoolroom extensive and terror-inspiring: "A huge bucket with water stood at one extremity of the room, and a clock of stupendous dimensions at the other." Thus the schoolboy Poe was haunted by the terrifying and prodigious presence of the clock which he confronted everywhere, both inside and outside the schoolroom, and which harassed him as much by its sullen and melodious "roar" as by the ambiguity of its twofold form (the church clock, the schoolroom clock, though in both cases "stupendous"). One senses from this the child's animosity against a being which terrorized him with its "sudden" chimings in addition to persecuting him with its slowness in the classroom where he languishes a *prisoner* of time.[1]

One must still inquire why the two clocks, to which other schoolboys would have given only superficial attention, impressed their presence so indelibly upon the imagination of the young Poe. We may answer this question with some assurance.

It has been observed that in the unconscious of the neurotic the rhythm of the clock is frequently associated with that of the sex act. It has also been observed that children who accidentally witness the sex act interpret it as a scene of struggle between the two partners. Finally we know that during his first years Poe was raised in a family of wandering players, whose poverty was so great that more than once, doubtlessly, in the course of their tours they must have had to content themselves with a single room for a lodging. Nothing argues against the assumption that little Edgar once chanced to witness the nocturnal romps of his parents and that his infant imagination would have mistaken their movements for combat, struggle. That misinterpretation would loom, confusedly, in the background of the clocks of Poe, imparting the character of an obsession to them. One passage from "The Devil in the Belfry" appears to corroborate this interpretation entirely: "Every now and then one might catch a glimpse of the scoundrel [the devil] through the smoke. There he sat in the belfry upon the belfry-man, who was lying flat upon his back." The superposition of the two hands symbolized by this occurrence in "The Devil in the Belfry" might also, therefore, in its turn, symbolize the sex act fleetingly glimpsed. The crazed clock which strikes thirteen just, one surmises, before stopping forever might reveal, then, the unconscious desire—colored by

---

[1] It is the same obsession, no doubt, which looms, as Poe himself avowed, behind the figure of the raven: "that bird, that imp bird," Poe said not long before the composition of the poem bearing the very title "The Raven," "pursued me, mentally, perpetually; I cannot rid myself of his presence; as I sit here, I hear its croak as I used to hear it at Stoke Newington [the school which provides the setting for 'William Wilson'] the flap of its wings in my ear. . . ." (Cf. Lauvrière, *Le Génie morbide d'Edgar Poe* [Paris: 1935], p. 112).

Oedipal feelings—to put an end to the imaginary struggle and put the combatants out of commission.

Viewed in this context of Poe's clock symbols, "The Raven" will reveal its curious and profound similarity to "The Devil in the Belfry."

"The Raven"

The tale we have just analyzed has yielded an identification: "the devil = the minute hand." In "The Raven" the bird is associated by the narrator with the devil: "bird or devil" (stanza 16). Is it possible that this bird is a symbol of a minute hand? Like that hand and like the imp in the belfry, the raven is black; moreover, the coat of the devil has a swallowtail, which makes him look like a bird. Let us see whether reading the identification "the raven = the hour hand" into the poem does not give it a satisfactory implicit meaning.

In the very first line one finds: "Once upon a midnight dreary. . . ." It is, then, midnight in "The Raven"—as it was high noon in "The Devil in the Belfry." Hence, one may expect to find the same incidents in the poem as in the short story: an "hour hand" overtakes some "minute hand," a vertical structure results from their conjunction, chimes and creakings follow and precede their superposition—as well as such details as might suggest a clock's being thrown out of order.

Indeed, the raven—the minute hand—"stepped" in and "Perched upon a bust of Pallas just above [the] chamber door." In the same way the imp had stepped into the belfry to sit upon the "belfry-man." The parallelism is the more striking because, just as the belfry-man keeps watch in the belfry, the bust of Pallas in some way keeps watch in the room.

At high noon, thirteen strokes heralded the appearance of the devil at the belfry. Similarly, the raven hardly perched himself upon the bust of Pallas (note in this case the verticality of the structure raven, bust, and door make together, corresponding to the verticality of the belfry, the symbol of noon) when the lugubrious refrain "Nevermore" is heard—like a melancholy bell—*eleven* times, this "Nevermore" which so apparently symbolized the inexorable flow of time.

Each stroke of the clock in "The Devil in the Belfry" is echoed by the inhabitants of the borough in a foreign accent which Poe emphasizes. One notes that there is a remarkable similarity between the counting of the strokes pronounced in English by these fantastic Hollanders and the words (themselves representing the strokes of the bell) uttered in English by the mythical bird.

We have already assumed that the theme of the clock reflects in its turn an ill-interpreted incident of Poe's early childhood. Is it not possible to infer from the recurrent thematic clock the theme of the sex act of the poet's dead parents?

In this connection we note the bust of the *goddess* upon which the diabolical bird perches; the "midnight dreary"; the drowsiness of the narrator who is napping (stanza 4); the gripping nostalgia conveyed by the poem which sings of love and death.

"The Scythe of Time" [2]

In this short story—often overlooked—a feminine character, Psyche Zenobia, having the rather unfortunate idea of sticking her head through a hole in a gigantic dial of a *cathedral clock,* is slowly guillotined by the minute hand. The sensations of Psyche, minutely described by Poe, are what first attract our attention here. "The eternal *click-clack, click-clack, click-clack* of the clock was the most melodious of music in my ears," declares the heroine of the tale. And further, "Then there were the great figures upon the dial plate—how intelligent, how intellectual, they all looked! And presently they took to dancing the Mazurka, and I think it was the figure V who performed the most to my satisfaction. She was evidently a lady of breeding. . . . She did the pirouette to admiration—whirling round upon her apex." [3]

---

[2] Entitled "The Scythe of Time" when it first appeared in *The American Museum,* this tale, which may be regarded as a part of "How to Write a Blackwood Article," subsequently appeared in the *Broadway Journal* with the title "A Predicament" and the subtitle "The Scythe of Time." American reprintings generally designate it "A Predicament," sometimes without the subtitle. [ED.]

[3] Poe is precise in stating that the beheading is completed at *"twenty-five minutes past five* in the afternoon." The meeting of the minute hand with the hour hand, the *decapitation* of the hour hand by the minute hand (which in fact appears to guillotine it slowly) takes place upon the dial plate of any clock at about *twenty-seven minutes past five.* So striking a coincidence cannot,

In this rather astonishing text, we may read "in plain language" the following significations: "music = the tick-tock of a clock"; "characters, more precisely dancing characters = the figures of the dial-plate"; hence it follows that the dial plate itself, vast and flat, may be identified with a ballroom.

We shall be able to use this deciphering to interpret "The Masque of the Red Death."

"The Masque of the Red Death"

Time and the clock pervade this tale. We must bear in mind the "gigantic clock of ebony," the pendulum, the monotonous tick-tock, the musical striking of the hours, which emanates from the most sinister room in the "castellated abbey." The striking of midnight introduces the most dramatic episode. And it is "within the shadow of the ebony clock" that the ghostly masquerader stands at the end of the tale. We shall see now what new light the preceding interpretations may shed upon the surface events related in the tale.

All doors of Prince Prospero's dwelling are strongly barricaded so as to leave no means of ingress to "the sudden impulses of despair"; this autonomy, this "autarky," immediately recalls that of the borough "What Time Is It?" and doubtlessly reveals the castle to be a clock or a dial plate; and the ball with its lavish pomp, compared to the dance in "The Scythe of Time," justifies the same conclusion.

---

of course, be attributed merely to chance; but neither can it be attributed to conscious choice; therefore it remains that it must be the work of Poe's creative unconscious. Besides, the remark which we have just made implies that the thematic pattern of the tale focuses upon the conjunction of the clock hands at "twenty-seven minutes past five," and that Psyche Zenobia symbolizes the hour hand. Many details are immediately clarified: the progressive annihilation of Psyche corresponds to her slow disappearance under the minute hand; the small stature of Psyche alludes to her identity as hour hand. The endless climb up the circular staircase which leads Psyche to the top of the belfry ("round and up, round and up, round and up") symbolizes the slow circular advance of the hour hand upon the dial; the soliloquies of Psyche after the beheading mean that her death is apparent only, that she will keep "running" in spite of her momentary eclipse. Psyche's *apparent* death "traumatically" symbolizes, then, her defeat in a struggle witnessed in childhood by Poe at some moment when he was only half awake.

We shall see further that "The Pit and the Pendulum" presents enough analogies with "The Scythe of Time" to be placed beside that short story in a common "topological" cycle, that of "twenty-seven minutes past five."

A crowd of figures stand upon the dial which is swept by two hands of a clock. If our identification of the castellated abbey isolated from the exterior world as the dial plate is of any value, we may expect to find among the characters of the tale symbols of the hands and numbers of a clock. Since it is a festive ball which has called the assemblage of courtiers together, we see them as dancers; indeed, in our examination of "The Scythe of Time" we have noted the equation "dancing figures = figures on the dial plate." Besides, the plot involves two principal characters, the prince and the phantom. Might they symbolize the two *hands?* In any event the phantom advances "with a slow and solemn movement," moves with "deliberate and stately step," with "solemn and *measured*" step, makes his way *"uninterruptedly,"* as if impelled by some kind of inner necessity: one must agree that this uninterrupted, measured, solemn, and slow gait accords strikingly with the slow, regular tempo of the *hour hand*.

In this case Prospero must represent the *minute hand,* and a conjunction must take place between the two, doubtlessly in the form of a struggle—as in "The Devil in the Belfry" (the brawl between the devil and the belfry-man), or in "The Scythe of Time" (the beheading of Psyche by the minute hand). In fact the tale which we now have before us ends in such a struggle. That Prospero is something of a blade, like a minute hand, the bare blade which he carries suggests at once. That he acts the part of the minute hand is apparent from the circuit he travels and from his speed: he moves successively through the same chambers which the Masque of the Red Death had traversed, but Prospero moves precipitously, not slowly. At the end of the tale "the tall figure" stands "erect and motionless, within the shadow of the ebony clock": the hour hand (the phantom) is indeed standing erect, like the belfry, another embodiment of the smaller hand, at about twelve o'clock. As for Prospero, he falls "prostrate in death" a few feet from the specter; from which we may conclude only that at *about* midnight the mechanism has been thrown out of order (life has retired from both the clock of ebony and from the castle, the clock symbol). Similarly the chiming of the belfrey had been thrown out of order and had sounded thirteen o'clock; and, in all likelihood, the raven's deranged chanting of "Nevermore" *eleven* times is yet another similar case.

Again we may note that, as Prospero represents the minute hand, that is to say the father, his murder reflects Poe's unconscious jealousy—which makes "The Masque of the Red Death" the most Oedipal of the tales of Poe.

"The Fall of the House of Usher"

The text of this story includes no allusion to the realm of clocks, but the characters, the action, and the plot correspond with such fidelity to those of the preceding tale that it appears beyond doubt that they symbolize the same aspect of the fundamental theme of the clock and, further, the same nocturnal traumatism.

Like the castle in "The Masque of the Red Death" and like the village Vondervotteimittiss, the House of Usher clearly represents the clock. Its *autarky* bears testimony to that (it can be compared to the autonomy of the castle and the borough): Roderick Usher (and probably Madeline, who is at the point of death) had "for many years . . . never ventured forth"; their claustration, which parallels that of Prospero's guests and that of the inhabitants of "What O'Clock Is It?" probably has the same meaning. Thus the symbolic meaning of each of the inhabitants of the clock house is clear. The "sentience" of the house due to "the method of collocation of [its] stones," is precisely that of a clock which, to the consciousness of a child, is a living and thinking being; the symmetry of the house and its reflection in the tarn (one can see in the water "the remodelled and inverted images of . . . the vacant and eye-like windows") is that of the circular dial and of its frame, the upper half of which appears to be a reflection of the lower half. The intimate and uncanny relationship between the house and the Ushers parallels that which exists between the clock and the hands that "dwell" in it and are wholly governed by its mechanism.

The fact that two characters appear in a context symbolizing the clock immediately suggests here, as in the preceding tales, the presence of two clock hands. Roderick is shaken by "an habitual trepidancy" which he cannot overcome; he is a musician: "His long improvised dirges will ring forever in my ears," writes the narrator, and we know what childhood memories of a melodious and lugubrious chiming his funereal improvisations actually echo. As for Roderick's speaking voice, it is of an "energetic concision," an "abrupt, weighty, unhurried, hollow-sounding enunciation"; it is a "leaden, self-balanced, and perfectly modulated guttural utterance." In this grating speech, "unhurried" and "self-balanced," one will easily recognize the abrupt, rhythmical tick-tock of a clock. Lady Madeline, Roderick's twin sister, can also be considered as the image of a clock hand upon a dial, merely by virtue of her likeness to her brother.

If the House of Usher is a clock, and those who dwell in it are two clock hands, we will not be surprised to find at the explicit level of the tale a plot similar in every respect to those of "The Devil in the Belfry" and "The Masque of the Red Death." The agon of the drama is in the semblance of a fray between the brother and the sister at the end of which the figure of Madeline *is superimposed* upon Roderick's: "with a low moaning cry, [she] *fell heavily inward upon the person of her brother,* and in her violent and now final death-agonies, bore him to the floor a corpse. . . ." This superposition, that of the two hands, plainly indicates the "conjunction of midnight."

As a matter of fact, the "topology" of the manor house proves here to be of some significance. The vault in which Roderick has temporarily laid his apparently dead sister is situated "immediately beneath the portion of the building in which was [the narrator's] sleeping apartment" where the final drama will take place. While the narrator talks with Roderick and reads with him a gloomy tale of chivalry, Madeline, who has succeeded in escaping, climbs from the vault to the room "immediately" above it. Does this climbing up not represent quite obviously that of the minute hand—once entombed at the lowest point on the dial—"6"—then rising through the left-hand side of the dial until it reaches the highest point on it, and diametrically opposed—"12"?

We must observe, finally, that when we apply the interpretations we have heretofore developed—autarky, duelers, final verticality, etc.—to "The Fall of the House of Usher" (which naturally ends with the destruction, that is to say the stopping, of the pendulum and the two hands), our analysis yields some new meanings. Thus the descent, the entombment, acquires the meaning of the descent of the clock hand toward the lower half of the dial. The premature burial, the apparent death followed by a new birth seem to symbolize the disappearance, then the reappearance of a clock hand on a clock face. In this perspective "Ligeia" acquires a paradoxically precise meaning.

Two other stories also deal with the "conjunction of twelve"; they both borrow their explicit plots from the realm of the sea; and, since we are treating a poet haunted by Oedipal memories, we are warranted in recalling here the classic equivalent, the sea = the mother.

"A Descent into the Maelström"

Let us rapidly sketch the site in which the action of this tale unfolds. Looking at the scene from the vantage point of a high rock, one sees the following islands: Vurrgh, Moskoe, Ambaaren, Iflesen, Hoeyholm, Kieldholm, Suarven, Buckholm, Otterholm, Flimen, Sandflesen, and Skarholm. "These are the true names of the places—but why it has been thought necessary to name them at all, is more than either you or I can understand."

It seems easy to understand "why" they are thus enumerated: *just because these isles,* if we take the trouble to count them, *total twelve.*

Does this duodecimal reference suggest a clock? If so, we should find a circular structure and correspondences to a clock's hands and movement. This structure, these correspondences do exist.

The whirl of the Maelström is indeed circular; and it is isolated from the outside world, it is "autarkic": the ocean "stood like a huge writhing wall between us and the horizon." As for the hands of the clock, they are reprsented by the two fishermen—brothers— who are driven into the abyss. In effect, these fishermen start to transit the circular "belt of surf that always surrounds the whirl of the Maelström: "How often we made the circuit of the belt it is impossible to say. We careered round and round. . . ." Next, one of the sailors disappears into the abyss never to be seen again: similarly the hour hand of a clock plunges towards the nadir of the dial, not to be seen for many hours by an observer who stares at the number twelve. In contrast, this sailor's companion, after his rapid plunge into the abyss, comes up to the surface; similarly Lady Madeline comes up from the vault towards the chamber situated directly above it; similarly after a brief plunge the minute hand comes rapidly up towards the apex of the dial at the end of an hour.

But why should we classify the story we are now analyzing among the "midday-midnight stories"? Let us reread our text carefully: from the beginning of the adventures—therefore very near the lip of a crator, very near the apex of the liquid dial—the two fishermen are involved in a *bout* of wrestling, a brief affray, a *confrontation:* "He let go his hold upon [a water cask] and made for the ring, from which, in the agony of his terror, he endeavored to force my hands. . . . I did not care, however, to contest the point with him." Since this confrontation of the two clock hands takes place in the upper part of the clock face towards its apex, we may infer that here, as in the stories we have previously interpreted, it symbolizes the meeting at twelve o'clock. The sustained roar, the shrill din of the Maelström, described at the beginning of the text, provides the "background music" which would then symbolize the fatal sounding of midnight or noon.

This tale differs, all things considered, from the others in that the confrontation and the sounding of twelve o'clock, instead of ending the story, opens it. But that detail apart, we easily discover the haunting images of Poe's clock, as well as the more archaic memory of the traumatism caused by his parents, conveyed this time in a setting of the sea—that is to say, of the mother.

"MS. Found in a Bottle"

Let us briefly recall the plot of this story. A disabled ship has been drifting for several days through the southern seas. "About *noon,* as nearly as we could guess, our attention was . . . arrested by the appearance of the sun." Similarly, the last mention of the time refers to its being "about midnight"—and since that moment time has somehow stopped for the hero of the drama.

In the thematic perspective of Poe's works, this *noon* evidently entails a "conjunction," an "affray," between two surrogate hands. And in point of fact, such an affray does not fail to come to pass. "At a terrific height directly above us . . . hovered a gigantic ship. . . ." Here is the great hand, the faster hand, the minute hand. This "gigantic" ship, in fact, proceeds "all sails unfurled," and her hull is "of a deep dingy black" (the color of the imp, of the raven, etc.). Predictably, the huge ship "bears down" upon the wretched hulk (the slow and short hour hand), hits her violently, and the latter is never heard of again. But an unforeseeable incident hurls the terrified narrator into the rigging of the ghost ship. We are henceforth presented in some way the "travel anecdotes" of a "passenger" upon the minute hand.

The castaway becomes aware that the ship is "whirling dizzily" in immense concentric circles. The ship, enclosed in "the blackness of eternal night," ceaselessly coasts "stupendous ramparts of ice," which look "like the walls of the universe." All these details, which recall the fluid walls delimiting the world of the Maelström, certainly symbolize the prominent *frame* that borders the clock face.

The captain speaks to himself; he murmurs, in a muffled voice, "some low peevish syllables in a foreign tongue." (Dutch? We recall that The Flying Dutchman is the source of the tale.) Could this be the tick-tock of a clock? In "The Devil in the Belfry" (where English is pronounced by Hollanders) and in "The Raven" (where "Nevermore" is pronounced by a bird) the language of the clock has a certain foreign ring.

The gigantic ship (the minute hand) glides rapidly upon the waters. Now, as we recall, the initial "conjunction," which caused the ship to sink, occurred, if we take into account the stopping of time, at about *noon*. The random course of the vessel, symbolizing, then, the progression of the minute hand towards the lower part of the dial, must terminate in the disappearance of the surrogate of the hand into the depths of the sea. And indeed this is what ultimately comes about: "The ship is quivering—oh God! and—going down."

But the descent of the hand towards the lower half of the dial will necessarily be followed by its ascent towards the apex of "twelve" (unless the clock is out of order). Indeed, some details in our story do suggest the later reappearance of the ship. Thus the narrator declares: "We are surely doomed to hover continually on the brink of eternity, without taking a final plunge into the abyss." The ship therefore would be doomed alternately to immerge and emerge, to plunge and surge up, after an interval, to the surface. In other words the ship seems eternally to give itself rebirth, in the manner of a clock hand which alternately sinks and rises.[4]

---

[4] I think it useless to give any detailed commentary on a rather large number of stories which manifestly belong to the same "midday-midnight" cycle: the

*   *   *

I am convinced that almost all Poe's tales, no less than the philosophy he expounded in *Eureka,* rest upon the foundation of the theme of the clock, which somehow constitutes an invisible mechanism which imperceptibly actualizes the patent motif of the stories. But the image of the clock that haunted the creative regions of Poe's unconscious seems to have proliferated into a multitude of aspects and elements. The "conjunction of twelve o'clock" is far from being the only aspect of the theme from which a bouquet of masterpieces might grow. Thus several tales could be gathered which would constitute a new cycle, that of the "successive chimes."

"The Tell-Tale Heart"

Twelve o'clock; then three o'clock—The associations of the clock are particularly apparent here. We notice in order: "every night about *midnight";* "It took me an hour to place my whole head within the opening"; "every night *just at midnight";* "every night, *just at twelve";* *"a watch's minute hand* moves more quickly than did mine"; "—just as I have done, night after night, hearkening to the death *watches* in the walls"; "a low, dull, quick sound, such as a *watch* makes when enveloped in cotton." And finally, a whole page devoted to the climactic crescendo of the ticking.

In a context so translucent, it is easy to discern the thematic meaning of the plot.

The murder is committed at midnight precisely. We have already discovered that "midnight," as used by Poe, signifies the superposi-

---

curious reader may verify for himself that in "Metzengerstein," for example, the horse which masters and murders its rider is at once the minute hand of the clock face and Poe's mother, who thus revenges herself upon the husband who has trodden upon her; the reader may note also that in "The Oblong Box" the coffin which sinks into the sea and surfaces again, as has been foreseen by the captain of the shipwrecked vessel, symbolizes the hand making the circuit of the clock face; in "Lionizing" the social climbing of Robert Jones and his fall similarly represent the ascent and the descent of the clock hand; again, in "The Murders in the Rue Morgue" the ape, scrambling up and down a wall, etc. In all these stories one will find, of course, affrays, vertical structures, reminders of the ticking and the chiming of time, as well as other features which mark them as belonging to the realm of the clock, the realm of the traumatic, nocturnal vision which appears to be the realm of the creative unconscious of Poe.

tion of the two hands. Thus we read that when "the old man's hour had come," . . . "in an instant I dragged him to the floor and pulled the heavy bed over him." The superposition of the bed (the murder weapon) and the old man thus symbolizes the overlaying of the minute hand (the bed, the murderer) *upon* the hour hand (the old man) which it covers entirely.

Between midnight and four o'clock the narrator dismembers the corpse and stores it under the floor. At some moment—to judge by the context, at about three o'clock—he rips up "three planks from the flooring of the chamber." These three planks clearly represent the Roman numeral III; and the presence of the corpse of the little man—the hour hand—in this place thus signifies *the hour hand's arrival at the numeral three.*

In order to complete the topology of three o'clock, the minute hand must rise at that very moment vertically, making a right angle with the hour hand. In fact, when the *three* "officers of the police" present themselves (we must note this insistence upon, this haunting recurrence of the numeral *three*) the narrator—who had already laid the body of his victim in, no doubt, a *horizontal* position, places his "own seat upon the very spot beneath which reposed the corpse of the victim." We have already seen that the role of the minute hand has been assumed by the murderer. The verticality of the chair upon which he sits suggests that the minute hand is at *twelve*—while the hour hand (the old man) is at *three*. And the position of the chair—"upon the very spot" where the victim lies horizontally—answers very precisely to the *right angle* made at three o'clock by the smaller and larger hand on a clock's dial. All the while, naturally, the murderer hears the tick-tock of the "tell-tale heart," which at length becomes "the hellish tattoo" ("louder—*louder*") and eventuates in cries which, as usual, can be recognized as the chimes of the clock.

Traumatically the tale assumes the coloration of Oedipal feelings —in the struggle between the hands (the parents), the narrator, that is to say Poe, takes the part of the father and *kills* the old man (the hour hand, that is to say the mother), after a long hesitation which may betray scruples and remorse. The posthumous vengeance of the victim symbolizes the repentance connected with Oedipal temptation so clearly that we need hardly dwell upon it. We must notice the role played by the bed in the murder.

* * *

We may easily decipher "The Black Cat," in which the murder and the posthumous punishment parallel those in "The Tell-Tale Heart," and in which two successive "midnights" are manifestly suggested by the superpositions and the vertical structures (the verticality of the hanged cat, the verticality of the hidden corpse, standing behind the wall, the stick of the narrator rapping upon the very place where he has just buried his wife in a vertical posture). But now we turn to another example of successive chimings, somewhat more complex, somewhat more difficult to interpret: the well-known tale "The Pit and the Pendulum."

"The Pit and the Pendulum"

Twenty-seven past five; then six o'clock—The association of the clock with this story is suggested quite explicitly, first by these words: "The sound of the inquisitorial voices [which] seemed merged in one dreary indeterminate hum . . . conveyed to my soul the idea of *revolution*—perhaps from its association in fancy with the burr of a mill-wheel"; then by the frequent references to hours, intervals, the flow of time: "The mode and the *hour* [of death] were all that occupied and distracted me"; "agitation of spirit kept me awake for *many long hours*"; "for some *minutes* this fact occasioned me a world of vain trouble"; "I watched it for some *minutes*"; "It might have been *half an hour, perhaps even an hour*"; etc. etc. But chiefly the famous pendulum of the story, as well as the fresco of which it seems at first to be a part, links the explicit realm of the tale to *that of the clock:* in one of the panels in the ceiling "a very singular figure riveted my whole attention. *It was a painted figure of Time* as he is commonly represented, save that, in lieu of a scythe, he held what, at a casual glance, I supposed to be *the pictured image of a huge pendulum,* such as we see on antique clocks."

The narrator finds himself in a prison, in a "dungeon," cut off from the rest of the world; and this "autonomy" is emphasized and reinforced by the following detail: "a fissure, about half an inch in width, extending entirely around the prison at the base of the walls, which thus appeared, and were *completely separated from the floor.*" The "autarky" of a space, inhabited by the characters of the tale, symbolizes in Poe's works, the clock dial. Such was the case in "The Devil in the Belfry," in "The Masque of the Red Death," in "The

Descent into the Maelström," etc. The dungeon would then be the dial of the clock; and, in this case, one must expect to find two moving characters astir within this "autarkic" space, the one slow and short, the other fast and long, respectively symbolizing the hour hand and the minute hand.

It seems certain that the pendulum of the tale is no other thing than the minute hand. At the outset, this may produce some misgivings. Ought we not to regard this object, itself obviously a part of a clock, merely as a pendulum? First, however, the pendulum is substituted for a "scythe" ("in lieu of a scythe, he held . . . a huge pendulum"), and one recalls that, in the story entitled "The Scythe of Time" the *minute hand* played the role of the scythe of time. Further, the speed and the movement of the pendulum are quite erratic: the trajectory it describes varies ceaselessly instead of repeating the same curve; its course is *varied* because it *descends constantly;* finally it is armed with an edge which makes it a veritable scimitar meant to cut the prisoner in two; in the same way the minute hand in "The Scythe of Time" had beheaded Psyche; in this execution it is easy to discern a variant of the victorious "struggle" of Poe's "minute hands" against "hour hands."

If the pendulum represents the minute hand, it is clear that the prisoner represents the shorter hour hand. Thus at the outset he is armed with a knife (as Prince Prospero was armed with a dagger in "The Masque of the Red Death") representing the tapering end of a clock hand. This knife he proposes to plunge into the wall of his cell—just as the end of the clock hand always takes aim at some part of the periphery of the dial. He explores the walls of the prison as the hand sweeps around the periphery of the dial. He places "a part of the hem from [his] robe . . . at right angles to the wall." He is lying at full length, his head at the pit situated in the center of the cell. In all his positions and movements, we will recognize those of the clock hand. Incontestably, we have here the slow hour hand. The movements of the prisoner are labored, slow, even illusory (as when he attempts to survey the dimensions of his cell, and is grossly deceived). Most of the time he lies still. And in his struggle against the pendulum he is destined to be overcome, his rescue being effected by a miracle.

The two hands (the pendulum, the prisoner) of the dial (the dungeon) must confront each other and do battle. In what part of the dial does this confrontation take place? In most of the tales it takes place at the summit, near the number "twelve"; but not so in "The Pit and the Pendulum." "Tall figures . . . lifted and bore" the prisoner "down—down—still down" and he senses "the mere idea of the interminableness of the descent." In other words the hour hand descends into the lower half of the dial. Not, certainly, into the lowest depths, represented habitually by the figure "6"; for at the very center of the underground prison gapes a yet deeper abyss, the pit, to the very verge of which the prisoner moves, though he does not plunge into it. Thus the confrontation of the pendulum, the minute hand (which also *descends* from above, that is to say, plunges in pursuit of the hour hand into the lower half of the dial) with the prisoner, the hour hand, will take place very near the number "six," though at a slight distance, and consequently *before six o'clock*. We may now be more precise: the minute hand overtakes the hour hand within a few seconds of five twenty-seven. This precise time then expresses in cryptic language the aborted execution of the prisoner by the pendulum as it skims across his chest.

It is remarkable that the execution of Psyche by the minute hand of a clock, which Poe explicitly compares to "the scythe of time," takes place at precisely the same minute. This double coincidence confirms our reading of the confrontation of five twenty-seven in Poe's thematic landscape; and, conversely, it warrants our analysis of "The Pit."

These *données* cast new light upon the end of the tale. Since the tale does not end with the conjunction of five twenty-seven, what follows must symbolize some event *subsequent* to that moment. The first reminder of the realm of the clock which may be noticed after the conjunction of the two hands at the bottom of the dial is the antipodal position of those hands at "six o'clock" with the concomitant chiming. The progressive opening of the angle made by the two hands as the minute hand hastens toward the number "12," is aptly represented by the gradual transformation of the dungeon which, from a square, shifts "its form into that of a lozenge" that becomes flatter and flatter and which, at the moment when the "blast of many trumpets" rings out, and the "harsh grating as of a thousand thunders" sounds (symbolizing, as usual in Poe, the chimes) tends to become a straight line, the prisoner being then very near the pit, that is to say very near the lowest part of the dial.

The rapid ascent of the pendulum, the delivery of the prisoner from the very verge of the abyss would signify thematically the ascension of both the minute hand and the hour hand after the period of their descent towards the number "6".

*   *   *

"Three o'clock" and "midnight" ("The Tell-Tale Heart"); "five twenty-seven" and "six o'clock" ("The Pit and the Pendulum"): to these topological tales we might add, for example (besides "The Black Cat"—the two midnights—and "The Casque of Amontillado," in which the man who is prematurely buried, standing, corresponds to the vertical corpse of "The Black Cat"); "Silence—A Fable" (vertical structure of six o'clock); "Shadow—A Parable" (the right angle of nine o'clock); "The Unparalleled Adventures of Hans Pfaall" (the vertical approach of the balloon to the moon at exactly *noon*, the descent towards the earth at the termination of which, just before his landing, six bags predictably fall); etc.

It is true that a clock does not merely indicate the time. It is also a "mechanical" contrivance made up of diverse parts: the weights, the pendulum, the wheels, the pinions.

Hence, for example, "Hop-Frog" and "The Gold Bug," which recount the descent and ascent of the *weights* of the clock; "The Business Man" (previously entitled "Peter Pendulum") which represents the rhythmical, tireless pace of its *pendulum*; or again, "The Premature Burial," "Berenice," "The Man That Was Used Up," which express in cryptic language *the disassembly of the mechanism of a clock.*

Thematically, Poe's work constitutes an autonomous, autarkic whole: each tale bears the deeply engraved imprint of a single childhood experience, the experience of the clock, which in its turn both masks and reveals an obsessive phantasm yet more profound and primal—a phantasm, however, that seldom unveils itself to the conscious aesthetic mind of the maker.

The unconscious poet of the clock, of its dial, of its hands, of its hours, of its weights, of its pendulum, of its steady, and uncanny movement, of its subtle life, of its temporary death, of its melancholy strokes, of its obsessive tick-tock—in such guise we see Edgar Poe, the maniac of time.

The House of Poe

by Richard Wilbur

A few weeks ago, in the *New York Times Book Review,* Mr. Saul Bellow expressed impatience with the current critical habit of finding symbols in everything. No self-respecting modern professor, Mr. Bellow observed, would dare to explain Achilles' dragging of Hector around the walls of Troy by the mere assertion that Achilles was in a bad temper. That would be too drearily obvious. No, the professor must say that the circular path of Achilles and Hector relates to the theme of circularity which pervades *The Iliad.*

In the following week's *Book Review,* a pedantic correspondent corrected Mr. Bellow, pointing out that Achilles did not, in Homer's *Iliad,* drag Hector's body around the walls of Troy; this perhaps invalidates the Homeric example, but Mr. Bellow's complaint remains, nevertheless, a very sensible one. We are all getting a bit tired, I think, of that laboriously clever criticism which discovers mandalas in Mark Twain, rebirth archetypes in Edwin Arlington Robinson, and fertility myths in everybody.

Still, we must not be carried away by our impatience, to the point of demanding that no more symbols be reported. The business of the critic, after all, is to divine the intention of the work, and to interpret the work in the light of that intention; and since some writers are intentionally symbolic, there is nothing for it but to talk about their symbols. If we speak of Melville, we must speak of symbols. If we speak of Hawthorne, we must speak of symbols. And as for Edgar Allan Poe, whose sesquicentennial year we are met to observe, I think we can make no sense about him until we consider his work—

"The House of Poe," by Richard Wilbur. Originally presented as a lecture at the Library of Congress under the auspices of the Gertrude Clarke Whittall Poetry and Literature Fund. From *Annivesary Lectures 1959.* © 1966 by Richard Wilbur. Reprinted by permission of the author and the Library of Congress.

and in particular his prose fiction—as deliberate and often brilliant allegory.

Not everyone will agree with me that Poe's work has an accessible allegorical meaning. Some critics, in fact, have refused to see any substance, allegorical or otherwise, in Poe's fiction, and have regarded his tales as nothing more than complicated machines for saying "boo." Others have intuited undiscoverable meanings in Poe, generally of an unpleasant kind: I recall one Freudian critic declaring that if we find Poe unintelligible we should congratulate ourselves, since if we *could* understand him it would be proof of our abnormality.

It is not really surprising that some critics should think Poe meaningless, or that others should suppose his meaning intelligible only to monsters. Poe was not a wide-open and perspicuous writer; indeed, he was a secretive writer both by temperament and by conviction. He sprinkled his stories with sly references to himself and to his personal history. He gave his own birthday of January 19 to his character William Wilson; he bestowed his own height and color of eye on the captain of the phantom ship in "MS. Found in a Bottle"; and the name of one of his heroes, Arthur Gordon Pym, is patently a version of his own. He was a maker and solver of puzzles, fascinated by codes, ciphers, anagrams, acrostics, hieroglyphics, and the Kabbala. He invented the detective story. He was fond of aliases; he delighted in accounts of swindles; he perpetrated the famous Balloon Hoax of 1844; and one of his most characteristic stories is entitled "Mystification." A man so devoted to concealment and deception and unraveling and detection might be expected to have in his work what Poe himself called "undercurrents of meaning."

And that is where Poe, as a critic, said that meaning belongs: not on the surface of the poem or tale, but below the surface as a dark undercurrent. If the meaning of a work is made overly clear—as Poe said in his "Philosophy of Composition"—if the meaning is brought to the surface and made the upper current of the poem or tale, then the work becomes bald and prosaic and ceases to be art. Poe conceived of art, you see, not as a means of giving imaginative order to earthly experience, but as a stimulus to unearthly visions. The work of literary art does not, in Poe's view, present the reader with a provisional arrangement of reality; instead, it seeks to disengage the reader's mind from reality and propel it toward the ideal. Now, since Poe thought the function of art was to set the mind soaring upward in what he called "a wild effort to reach the Beauty above," it was important to him that the poem or tale should not have such definiteness and completeness of meaning as might contain the reader's mind within the work. Therefore Poe's criticism places a positive value on the obscuration of meaning, on a dark suggestiveness, on a deliberate vagueness by means of which the reader's mind may be set adrift toward the beyond.

Poe's criticism, then, assures us that his work does have meaning. And Poe also assures us that this meaning is not on the surface but in the depths. If we accept Poe's invitation to play detective, and commence to read him with an eye for submerged meaning, it is not long before we sense that there *are* meanings to be found, and that in fact many of Poe's stories, though superficially dissimilar, tell the same tale. We begin to have this sense as we notice Poe's repeated use of certain narrative patterns; his repetition of certain words and phrases; his use, in story after story, of certain scenes and properties. We notice, for instance, the recurrence of the *spiral* or *vortex*. In "Ms. Found in a Bottle," the story ends with a plunge into a whirlpool; the "Descent into the Maelström" also concludes in a watery vortex; the house of Usher, just before it plunges into the tarn, is swaddled in a whirlwind; the hero of "Metzengerstein," Poe's first published story, perishes in "a whirlwind of chaotic fire"; and at the close of "King Pest," Hugh Tarpaulin is cast into a puncheon of ale and disappears "amid a whirlpool of foam." That Poe offers us so many spirals or vortices in his fiction, and that they should always appear at the same terminal point in their respective narratives, is a strong indication that the spiral had some symbolic value for Poe. And it did: What the spiral invariably represents in any tale of Poe's is the loss of consciousness, and the descent of the mind into sleep.

I hope you will grant, before I am through, that to find spirals in Poe is not so silly as finding circles in Homer. The professor who finds circles in Homer does so to the neglect of more important and more provable meanings. But the spiral or vortex is a part of that symbolic language in which Poe said his say, and unless we understand it we cannot understand Poe.

But now I have gotten ahead of myself, and before I proceed with my project of exploring one area of Poe's symbolism, I think I had better say something about Poe's conception of poetry and the poet.

Poe conceived of God as a poet. The universe, therefore, was an artistic creation, a poem composed by God. Now, if the universe is a poem, it follows that the one proper response to it is aesthetic, and that God's creatures are attuned to Him in proportion as their imaginations are ravished by the beauty and harmony of his creation. Not to worship beauty, not to regard poetic knowledge as divine, would be to turn one's back on God and fall from grace.

The planet Earth, according to Poe's myth of the cosmos, has done just this. It has fallen away from God by exalting the scientific reason above poetic intuition, and by putting its trust in material fact rather than in visionary knowledge. The Earth's inhabitants are thus corrupted by rationalism and materialism; their souls are diseased; and Poe sees this disease of the human spirit as having contaminated physical nature. The woods and fields and waters of Earth have thereby lost their first beauty, and no longer clearly express God's imagination; the landscape has lost its original perfection of composition, in proportion as men have lost their power to perceive the beautiful.

Since Earth is a fallen planet, life upon Earth is necessarily a torment for the poet: neither in the human sphere nor in the realm of nature can he find fit objects for contemplation, and indeed his soul is oppressed by everything around him. The rationalist mocks at him; the dull, prosaic spirit of the age damps his imaginative spark; the gross materiality of the world crowds in upon him. His only recourse is to abandon all concern for Earthly things, and to devote himself as purely as possible to unearthly visions, in hopes of glimpsing that heavenly beauty which is the thought of God.

Poe, then, sees the poetic soul as at war with the mundane physical world; and that warfare is Poe's fundamental subject. But the war between soul and world is not the only war. There is also warfare within the poet's very nature. To be sure, the poet's nature was not always in conflict with itself. Prior to his earthly incarnation, and during his dreamy childhood, Poe's poet enjoyed a serene unity of being; his consciousness was purely imaginative, and he knew the universe for the divine poem that it is. But with his entrance into adult life, the poet became involved with a fallen world in which the physical, the factual, the rational, the prosaic are not escapable. Thus, compromised, he lost his perfect spirituality, and is now cursed with a divided nature. Though his imagination still yearns toward ideal beauty, his mortal body chains him to the physical and temporal and local; the hungers and passions of his body draw him toward external objects, and the conflict of conscience and desire degrades and distracts his soul; his mortal senses try to convince him of the reality of a material world which his soul struggles to escape; his reason urges him to acknowledge everyday fact, and to confine his thought within the prison of logic. For all these reasons it is not easy for the poet to detach his soul from earthly things, and regain his lost imaginative power—his power to commune with that supernal beauty which is symbolized, in Poe, by the shadowy and angelic figures of Ligeia, and Helen, and Lenore.

These, then, are Poe's great subjects: first, the war between the poetic soul and the external world; second, the war between the poetic soul and the earthly self to which it is bound. All of Poe's major stories are allegorical presentations of these conflicts, and everything he wrote bore somehow upon them.

How does one wage war against the external world? And how does one release one's visionary soul from the body, and from the constraint of the reason? These may sound like difficult tasks; and yet we all accomplish them every night. In a subjective sense—and Poe's thought is wholly subjective—we destroy the world every time we close our eyes. If *esse est percipi,* as Bishop Berkeley said—if to be is to be perceived—then when we withdraw our attention from the world in somnolence or sleep, the world ceases to be. As our minds move toward sleep, by way of drowsiness and reverie and the hypnagogic state, we escape from consciousness of the world, we escape from awareness of our bodies, and we enter a realm in which reason no longer hampers the play of the imagination: we enter the realm of dream.

Like many romantic poets, Poe identified imagination with dream. Where Poe differed from other romantic poets was in the literalness and absoluteness of the identification, and in the clinical precision with which he observed the phenomena of dream, carefully distinguishing the various states through which the mind passes on its way to sleep. A large number of Poe's stories derive their very structure from this sequence of mental states: "Ms. Found in a Bottle," to give but one example, is an allegory of the mind's voyage from the waking world into the world of dreams, with each main step of the narrative symbolizing the passage of the mind from one state to another—from wakefulness to reverie, from reverie to the hypnagogic state, from the hypnagogic state to the deep dream. The departure of the narrator's ship from Batavia represents the mind's withdrawal from the waking world; the drowning of the captain and all but one of the crew represents the growing solitude of reverie; when the narrator is transferred by collision from a real ship to a phantom ship, we are to understand that he has passed from reverie, a state in which reality and dream exist in a kind of equilibrium, into the free fantasy of the hypnagogic state. And when the phantom ship makes its final plunge into the whirlpool, we are to understand that the narrator's mind has gone over the brink of sleep and descended into dreams.

What I am saying by means of this example is that the scenes and situations of Poe's tales are always concrete representations of states of mind. If we bear in mind Poe's fundamental plot—the effort of the poetic soul to escape all consciousness of the world in dream—we soon recognize the significance of certain scenic or situational motifs which turn up in story after story. The most important of these recurrent motifs is that of *enclosure* or *circumscription;* perhaps the latter term is preferable, because it is Poe's own word, and because Poe's enclosures are so often more or less circular in form. The heroes of Poe's tales and poems are violently circumscribed by whirlpools, or peacefully circumscribed by cloud-capped Paradisal valleys; they float upon circular pools ringed in by steep flowering hillsides; they dwell on islands, or voyage to them; we find Poe's heroes also in coffins, in the cabs of balloons, or hidden away in the holds of ships; and above all we find them sitting alone in the claustral and richly furnished rooms of remote and mouldering mansions.

Almost never, if you think about it, is one of Poe's heroes to be seen standing in the light of common day; almost never does the Poe hero breathe the air that others breathe; he requires some kind of envelope in order to be what he is; he is always either enclosed or on his way to an enclosure. The narrative of William Wilson conducts the hero from Stoke Newington to Eton, from Eton to

Oxford, and then to Rome by way of Paris, Vienna, Berlin, Moscow, Naples, and Egypt: and yet, for all his travels, Wilson seems never to set foot out-of-doors. The story takes place in a series of rooms, the last one locked from the inside.

Sometimes Poe emphasizes the circumscription of his heroes by multiple enclosures. Roderick Usher dwells in a great and crumbling mansion from which, as Poe tells us, he has not ventured forth in many years. This mansion stands islanded in a stagnant lake, which serves it as a defensive moat. And beyond the moat lies the Usher estate, a vast barren tract having its own peculiar and forbidding weather and atmosphere. You might say that Roderick Usher is defended in depth; and yet at the close of the story Poe compounds Roderick's inaccessibility by having the mansion and its occupant swallowed up by the waters of the tarn.

What does it mean that Poe's heroes are invariably enclosed or circumscribed? The answer is simple: circumscription, in Poe's tales, means the exclusion from consciousness of the so-called real world, the world of time and reason and physical fact; it means the isolation of the poetic soul in visionary reverie or trance. When we find one of Poe's characters in a remote valley, or a claustral room, we know that he is in the process of dreaming his way out of the world.

Now, I want to devote the time remaining to the consideration of one kind of enclosure in Poe's tales: the mouldering mansion and its richly furnished rooms. I want to concentrate on Poe's architecture and décor for two reasons: first, because Poe's use of architecture is so frankly and provably allegorical that I *should* be able to be convincing about it; second, because by concentrating on one area of Poe's symbolism we shall be able to see that his stories are allegorical not only in their broad patterns, but also in their smallest details.

Let us begin with a familiar poem, "The Haunted Palace." The opening stanzas of this poem, as a number of critics have noted, make a point-by-point comparison between a building and the head of a man. The exterior of the palace represents the man's physical features; the interior represents the man's mind engaged in harmonious imaginative thought.

> In the greenest of our valleys
> By good angels tenanted,

Once a fair and stately palace—
  Radiant palace—reared its head.
In the monarch Thought's dominion—
  It stood there!
Never seraph spread a pinion
  Over fabric half so fair!

Banners yellow, glorious, golden,
  On its roof did float and flow,
(This—all this—was in the olden
  Time long ago,)
And every gentle air that dallied,
  In that sweet day,
Along the ramparts plumed and pallid,
  A wingéd odor went away.

Wanderers in that happy valley,
  Through two luminous windows, saw
Spirits moving musically,
  To a lute's well-tunéd law,
Round about a throne where, sitting,
  Porphyrogene,
In state his glory well befitting,
  The ruler of the realm was seen.

And all in pearl and ruby glowing
  Was the fair palace door,
Through which came flowing, flowing, flowing,
  And sparkling evermore,
A troop of Echoes, whose sweet duty
  Was but to sing,
In voices of surpassing beauty,
  The wit and wisdom of their king.

I expect you observed that the two luminous windows of the palace are the eyes of a man, and that the yellow banners on the roof are his luxuriant blond hair. The "pearl and ruby" door is the man's mouth—ruby representing red lips, and pearl representing pearly white teeth. The beautiful Echoes which issue from the pearl and ruby door are the poetic utterances of the man's harmonious imagination, here symbolized as an orderly dance. The angel-guarded valley in which the palace stands, and which Poe describes as "the monarch Thought's dominion," is a symbol of the man's exclusive awareness of exalted and spiritual things. The valley is what Poe elsewhere called "that evergreen and radiant paradise which the true poet knows . . . as the limited realm of his authority, as the circumscribed Eden of his dreams."

As you all remember, the last two stanzas of the poem describe the physical and spiritual corruption of the palace and its domain, and it was to this part of the poem that Poe was referring when he told a correspondent, "By the 'Haunted Palace' I mean to imply a mind haunted by phantoms—a disordered brain." Let me read you the closing lines:

> But evil things, in robes of sorrow,
>   Assailed the monarch's high estate.
> (Ah, let us mourn!—for never morrow
>   Shall dawn upon him desolate!)
> And round about his home the glory
>   That blushed and bloomed,
> Is but a dim-remembered story
>   Of the old time entombed.
>
> And travellers, now, within that valley,
>   Through the red-litten windows see
> Vast forms, that move fantastically
>   To a discordant melody,
> While, like a ghastly rapid river,
>   Through the pale door
> A hideous throng rush out forever
>   And laugh—but smile no more.

The domain of the monarch Thought, in these final stanzas, is disrupted by civil war, and in consequence everything alters for the worse. The valley becomes barren, like the domain of Roderick Usher; the eye-like windows of the palace are no longer "luminous," but have become "red-litten"—they are like the bloodshot eyes of a madman or a drunkard. As for the mouth of our allegorized man, it is now "pale" rather than "pearl and ruby," and through it come no sweet Echoes, as before, but the wild laughter of a jangling and discordant mind.

The two states of the palace—before and after—are, as we can see, two states of mind. Poe does not make it altogether clear *why* one state of mind has given way to the other, but by recourse to similar tales and poems we can readily find the answer. The palace in its original condition expresses the imaginative harmony which the poet's soul enjoys in early childhood, when all things are viewed with a tyrannical and unchallenged subjectivity. But as the soul passes from childhood into adult life, its consciousness is more and more invaded by the corrupt and corrupting external world: it succumbs to passion, it develops a conscience, it makes concessions to reason and to objective fact. Consequently, there is civil war in the palace of the mind. The imagination must now struggle against the intellect and the moral sense; finding itself no longer able to possess the world through a serene solipsism, it strives to annihilate the outer world by turning in upon itself; it flees into irrationality and dream; and all its dreams are efforts both to recall and to simulate its primal, unfallen state. "The Haunted Palace" presents us with a possible key to the general meaning of Poe's architecture; and this key proves, if one tries it, to open every building in Poe's fiction. Roderick Usher, as you will remember, declaims "The Haunted Palace" to the visitor who tells his story, accompanying the poem with wild improvisations on the guitar. We are encouraged, therefore, to compare the palace of the poem with the house of the story; and it is no surprise to find that the Usher mansion has "vacant eye-like windows," and that there are mysterious physical sympathies between Roderick Usher and the house in which he dwells. The House of Usher *is*, in allegorical fact, the physical body of Roderick Usher, and its dim interior *is*, in fact, Roderick Usher's visionary mind.

The House of Usher, like many edifices in Poe, is in a state of extreme decay. The stonework of its facade has so crumbled and decomposed that it reminds the narrator, as he puts it, "of the specious totality of old wood-work which has rotted for long years in some neglected vault." The Usher mansion is so eaten away, so fragile, that it seems a breeze would push it over; it remains standing only because the atmosphere of Usher's domain is perfectly motionless and dead. Such is the case also with the "time-eaten towers that tremble not" in Poe's poem "The City in the Sea"; and likewise the magnificent architecture of "The Domain of Arnheim" is said to "sustain itself by a miracle in mid-air." Even the detective Dupin lives in a perilously decayed structure: the narrator of "The Murders in the Rue Morgue" tells how he and Dupin dwelt in a "time-eaten and grotesque mansion, long deserted through superstitions into which we did not enquire, and tottering to its fall in a retired and desolate portion of the Faubourg St. Germain." (Notice how, even when Poe's buildings are situated in cities, he manages to circumscribe them with a protective desolation.)

We must now ask what Poe means by the extreme and tottering decay of so many of his structures. The answer is best given by reference to "The Fall of the House of Usher," and in giving the answer we shall arrive, I think, at an understanding of the pattern of that story.

"The Fall of the House of Usher" is a journey into the depths of the self. I have said that all journeys in Poe are allegories of the process of dreaming, and we must understand "The Fall of the House of Usher" as a dream of the narrator's, in which he leaves behind him the waking, physical world and journeys inward toward his *moi intérieur,* toward his inner and spiritual self. That inner and spiritual self is Roderick Usher.

Roderick Usher, then, is a part of the narrator's self, which the narrator reaches by way of reverie. We may think of Usher, if we like, as the narrator's imagination, or as his visionary soul. Or we may think of him as a *state of mind* which the narrator enters at a certain stage of his progress into dreams. Considered as a state of mind, Roderick Usher is an allegorical figure representing the hypnagogic state.

The hypnagogic state, about which there is strangely little said in the literature of psychology, is a condition of semi-consciousness in which the closed eye beholds a continuous procession of vivid and constantly changing forms. These forms sometimes have color, and are often abstract in character. Poe regarded the hypnagogic state as the visionary condition *par excellence,* and he considered its rapidly shifting abstract images to be—as he put it—"glimpses of the spirit's outer world." These visionary glimpses, Poe says in one of his *Marginalia,* "arise in the soul . . . only . . . at those mere points of time where the confines of the waking world blend with those of the world of dreams." And Poe goes on to say: "I am aware of these 'fancies' only when I am upon the very brink of sleep, with the consciousness that I am so."

Roderick Usher enacts the hypnagogic state in a number of ways. For one thing, the narrator describes Roderick's behavior as inconsistent, and characterized by constant alternation: he is alternately vivacious and sullen; he is alternately communicative and rapt; he speaks at one moment with "tremulous indecision," and at the next with the "energetic concision" of an excited opium-eater. His conduct resembles, in other words, that wavering between consciousness and subconsciousness which characterizes the hypnagogic state. The trembling of Roderick's body, and the floating of his silken hair, also bring to mind the instability and underwater quality of hypnagogic images. His improvisations on the guitar suggest hypnagogic experience in their rapidity, changeableness, and wild novelty. And as for Usher's paintings, which the narrator describes as "pure abstractions," they quite simply *are* hypnagogic images. The narrator says of Roderick, "From the paintings over which his elaborate fancy brooded, and which grew, touch by touch, into vaguenesses at which I shuddered the more thrillingly because I shuddered without knowing why—from these paintings (vivid as their images now are before me) I would in vain endeavor to educe more than a small portion which should lie within the compass of merely written words." That the narrator finds Roderick's paintings indescribable is interesting, because in that one of the *Marginalia* from which I have quoted, Poe asserts that the only things in human experience which lie "beyond the compass of words" are the visions of the hypnagogic state.

Roderick Usher stands for the hypnagogic state, which as Poe said is a teetering condition of mind occurring "upon the very brink of sleep." Since Roderick is the embodiment of a state of mind in which *falling*—falling asleep—is imminent, it is appropriate that the building which symbolizes his mind should promise at every moment to fall. The House of Usher stares down broodingly at its reflection in the tarn below, as in the hypnagogic state the conscious mind may stare into the subconscious; the house threatens continually to collapse because it is extremely easy for the mind to slip from the hypnagogic state into the depths of sleep; and when the House of Usher *does* fall, the story ends, as it must, because the mind, at the end of its inward journey, has plunged into the darkness of sleep.

We have found one allegorical meaning in the tottering decay of Poe's buildings; there is another meaning, equally important, which may be stated very briefly. I have said that Poe saw the poet as at war with the material world, and with the material or physical aspects of himself; and I have said that Poe identified poetic imagination with the power to escape from the material and the materialistic, to exclude them from consciousness and so subjectively destroy them. Now, if we recall these things, and recall also that the exteriors of Poe's houses or palaces, with their eye-like windows and mouth-like doors, represent the physical features of Poe's dreaming heroes, then the characteristic dilapidation of Poe's architecture takes on sudden significance. The extreme decay of the House of Usher—a decay so extreme as to approach the atmospheric—is quite simply a sign that the narrator, in reaching that state of mind which he calls Roderick Usher, has very nearly dreamt himself free of his physical body, and of the material world with which that body connects him.

This is what decay or decomposition mean everywhere in Poe; and we find them almost everywhere. Poe's preoccupation with decay is not, as some critics have thought, an indication of necrophilia; decay in Poe is a symbol of visionary remoteness from the physical, a sign that the state of mind represented is one of almost pure spirituality. When the House of Usher disintegrates or dematerializes at the close of the story, it does so because Roderick Usher has become all soul. "The Fall of the House of Usher," then, is not really a horror story; it is a triumphant report by the narrator that it *is* possible for the poetic soul to shake off this temporal, rational, physical world and escape, if only for a moment, to a realm of unfettered vision.

We have now arrived at three notions about Poe's typical building. It is set apart in a valley or a sea or a waste place, and this remoteness is intended to express the retreat of the poet's mind from worldly consciousness into dream. It is a tottery structure, and this indicates that the dreamer within is in that unstable threshold condition called the hypnagogic state. Finally, Poe's typical building is crumbling or decomposing, and this means that the dreamer's mind is moving toward a perfect freedom from his material self and the material world. Let us now open the door—or mouth—of Poe's building and visit the mind inside.

As we enter the palace of the visionary hero of "The Assignation," or the house of Roderick Usher, we find ourselves approaching the master's private chamber by way of dim and winding passages, or a winding staircase. There is no end to dim windings in Poe's fiction: there are dim and winding woods paths, dim and winding streets, dim and winding watercourses—and, whenever the symbolism is architectural, there are likely to be dim and winding passages or staircases. It is not at all hard to guess what Poe means by this symbol. If we think of waking life as dominated by reason, and if we think of the reason as a daylight faculty which operates in straight lines, then it is proper that reverie should be represented as an obscure and wandering movement of the mind. There are other, and equally obvious meanings in Poe's symbol of dim and winding passages: to grope through such passages is to become confused as to place and direction, just as in reverie we begin to lose any sense of locality, and to have an infinite freedom in regard to space. In his description of the huge old mansion in which William Wilson went to school, Poe makes this meaning of winding passages very plain:

> But the house!—how quaint an old building was this!—to me how veritable a palace of enchantment! There was no end to its windings —to its incomprehensible subdivisions. It was difficult, at any given time, to say with certainty upon which of its two stories one happened to be. From each room to every other there were sure to be found three or four steps either in ascent or descent. Then the lateral branches were innumerable—inconceivable—and so returning in upon themselves, that our most exact ideas in regard to the whole mansion were not very far different from those with which we pondered on infinity.

Dim windings indicate the state of reverie; they point toward that infinite freedom in and from space which the mind achieves in dreams; also, in their curvature and in their occasional doubling-back, they anticipate the mind's final spiralling plunge into unconsciousness. But the immediate goal of reverie's winding passages is that magnificent chamber in which we find the visionary hero slumped in a chair or lolling on an ottoman, occupied in purging his consciousness of everything that is earthly.

Since I have been speaking of geometry—of straight lines and curves and spirals—perhaps the first thing to notice about Poe's dream rooms is their shape. It has already been said that the enclosures of Poe's tales incline to a curving or circular form. And Poe himself, in certain of his essays and dialogues, explains this inclination by denouncing what he calls "the harsh mathematical reason of the schools," and complaining that practical science has covered the face of the earth with "rectangular obscenities." Poe quite explicitly identifies regular angular forms with everyday reason, and the circle, oval, or fluid arabesque with the otherworldly imagination. Therefore, if we discover that the dream chambers of Poe's fiction are free of angular regularity, we may be sure that we are noticing a pointed and purposeful consistency in his architecture and décor.

The ball-room of the story "Hop-Frog" is circular. The Devil's apartment in "The Duc de l'Omelette" has its corners "rounded into niches," and we find rounded corners also in Poe's essay "The Philosophy of Furniture." In "Ligeia," the bridal chamber is a pentagonal turret room; however, the angles are concealed by sarcophagi, so that the effect is circular. The corners of Roderick Usher's chamber are likewise concealed, being lost in deep shadow. Other dream rooms are either irregular or indeterminate in form. For example, there are the seven rooms of Prince Prospero's imperial suite in "The Masque of the Red Death." As Poe observes, "in many palaces . . . such suites form a long and straight vista"; but in Prince Prospero's palace, as he describes it, "the apartments were so irregularly disposed that the vision embraced but little more than one at a time. There was a sharp turn at every twenty or thirty yards, and at each turn a novel effect." The turret room of *The Oval Portrait* is not defined as to shape; we are told, however, that it is architecturally "bizarre," and complicated by a quantity of unexpected nooks and niches. Similarly, the visionary's apartment in "The Assignation" is described only as dazzling, astounding and original in its architecture; we are not told in what way its dimensions are peculiar, but it seems safe to assume that it would be a difficult room to measure for wall-to-wall carpeting. The room of "The Assignation," by the way—like that of "Ligeia"—has its walls enshrouded in rich figured draperies which are continually agitated by some mysterious agency. The fluid shifting of the figures suggests, of course, the behavior of hypnagogic images; but the agitation of the draperies would also produce a perpetual ambiguity of architectural form, and the effect would resemble that which Pevsner ascribes to the interior of San Vitale in Ravenna: "a sensation of uncertainty [and] of a dreamlike floating."

Poe, as you see, is at great pains to avoid depicting the usual squarish sort of room in which we spend much of our waking lives. His chambers of dream either approximate the circle—an infinite form which is, as Poe somewhere observes, "the emblem of Eternity" —or they so lack any apprehensible regularity of shape as to suggest the changeableness and spatial freedom of the dreaming mind. The exceptions to this rule are few and entirely explainable. I will grant, for instance, that the iron-walled torture chamber of "The Pit and the Pendulum" portrays the very reverse of spatial freedom, and that it is painfully angular in character, the angles growing more acute as the torture intensifies. But there is very good allegorical reason for these things. The rooms of "Ligeia" or "The Assignation" symbolize a triumphantly imaginative state of mind in which the dreamer is all but free of the so-called "real" world. In "The Pit and the Pendulum," the dream is of quite another kind; it is a nightmare state, in which the dreamer is imaginatively impotent, and can find no refuge from reality, even in dream. Though he lies on the brink of the pit, on the very verge of the plunge into unconsciousness, he is still unable to disengage himself from the physical and temporal world. The physical oppresses him in the shape of lurid graveyard visions; the temporal oppresses him in the form of an enormous and deadly pendulum. It is altogether appropriate, then, that this particular chamber should be constricting and cruelly angular.

But let us return to Poe's typical room, and look now at its furnishings. They are generally weird, magnificent, and suggestive of great wealth. The narrator of "The Assignation," entering the hero's apartment, feels "blind and dizzy with luxuriousness," and looking about him he confesses, "I could not bring myself to believe that the wealth of any subject in Europe could have supplied the princely magnificence which burned and blazed around." Poe's visionaries are, as a general thing, extremely rich; the hero of "Ligeia" confides that, as for wealth, he possesses "far more, very far more, than ordinarily falls to the lot of mortals"; and Ellison, in "The Domain of Arnheim," is the fortunate inheritor of 450 million dollars. Legrand, in "The Gold Bug," with his treasure of 450 *thousand,* is only a poor relation of Mr. Ellison; still, by ordinary standards, he seems sublimely solvent.[1]

---

[1] In writing the above, I misremembered the amount of Legrand's treasure. The sum mentioned is the estimated value of the coins only, whereas the treasure's total value was in excess of "a million and a half of dollars." [R. W., 1966].

Now, we must be careful to take all these riches in an allegorical sense. As we contemplate the splendor of any of Poe's rooms, we must remember that the room is a state of mind, and that everything in it is therefore a thought, a mental image. The allegorical meaning of the costliness of Poe's décor is simply this: that his heroes are richly imaginative. And since imagination is a gift rather than an acquisition, it is appropriate that riches in Poe should be inherited or found, but never earned.

Another thing we notice about Poe's furnishings is that they are eclectic in the extreme. Their richness is not the richness of Tiffany's and Sloan's, but of all periods and all cultures. Here is a partial inventory of the fantastic bridal-chamber in "Ligeia": Egyptian carvings and sarcophagi; Venetian glass; fretwork of a semi-Gothic, semi-Druidical character; a Saracenic chandelier; Oriental ottomans and candelabra; an Indian couch; and figured draperies with Norman motifs. The same defiance of what interior decorators once called "keeping" is found in the apartment of the visionary hero of "The Assignation," and one of that hero's speeches hints at the allegorical meaning of his jumbled décor:

> To dream [says the hero of "The Assignation"]—to dream has been the business of my life. I have therefore framed for myself, as you see, a bower of dreams. In the heart of Venice could I have erected a better? You behold around you, it is true, a medley of architectural embellishments. The chastity of Ionia is offended by antediluvian devices, and the sphynxes of Egypt are outstretched upon carpets of gold. Yet the effect is incongruous to the timid alone. Proprieties of place, and especially of time, are the bugbears which terrify mankind from the contemplation of the magnificent.

That last sentence, with its scornful reference to "proprieties of place, and . . . time," should put us in mind of the first stanza of Poe's poem "Dream-Land":

> By a route obscure and lonely,
> Haunted by ill angels only,
> Where an Eidolon, named NIGHT,
> On a black throne reigns upright,
> I have reached these lands but newly
> From an ultimate dim Thule—
> From a wild weird clime that lieth, sublime,
> Out of SPACE—out of TIME.

In dream-land, we are "out of SPACE—out of TIME," and the same is true of such apartments or "bowers of dreams" as the hero of "The Assignation" inhabits. His eclectic furnishings, with their wild juxtapositions of Venetian and Indian, Egyptian and Norman, are symbolic of the visionary soul's transcendence of spatial and temporal limitations. When one of Poe's dream-rooms is *not* furnished in the fashion I have been describing, the idea of spatial and temporal freedom is often conveyed in some other manner: Roderick Usher's library, for instance, with its rare and precious volumes belonging to all times and tongues, is another concrete symbol of the timelessness and placelessness of the dreaming mind.

We have spoken of the winding approaches to Poe's dream chambers, of their curvilinear or indeterminate shape, and of the rich eclecticism of their furnishings. Let us now glance over such matters as lighting, soundproofing, and ventilation. As regards lighting, the rooms of Poe's tales are never exposed to the naked rays of the sun, because the sun belongs to the waking world and waking consciousness. The narrator of "The Murders in the Rue Morgue" tells how he and his friend Dupin conducted their lives in such a way as to avoid all exposure to sunlight. "At the first dawn of the morning," he writes, "we closed all the massy shutters of our old building; lighting a couple of tapers which, strongly perfumed, threw out only the ghastliest and feeblest of rays. By the aid of these we then busied our souls in dreams . . ."

In some of Poe's rooms, there simply are no windows. In other cases, the windows are blocked up or shuttered. When the windows are not blocked or shuttered, their panes are tinted with a crimson or leaden hue, so as to transform the light of day into a lurid or ghastly glow. This kind of lighting, in which the sun's rays are admitted but transformed, belongs to the portrayal of those half-states of mind in which dream and reality are blended. Filtered through tinted panes, the sunlight enters certain of Poe's rooms as it might enter the half-closed eyes of a daydreamer, or the dream-dimmed eyes of someone awakening from sleep. But when Poe wishes to represent that deeper phase of dreaming in which visionary consciousness has all but annihilated any sense of the external world, the lighting is always artificial and the time is always night.

Flickering candles, wavering torches, and censers full of writhing varicolored flames furnish much of the illumination of Poe's rooms,

and one can see the appropriateness of such lighting to the vague
and shifting perceptions of the hypnagogic state. But undoubtedly
the most important lighting-fixture in Poe's rooms—and one which
appears in a good half of them—is the chandelier. It hangs from the
lofty ceiling by a long chain, generally of gold, and it consists sometimes of a censer, sometimes of a lamp, sometimes of candles, sometimes of a glowing jewel (a ruby or a diamond), and once, in the
macabre tale "King Pest," of a skull containing ignited charcoal.
What we must understand about this chandelier, as Poe explains
in his poem "Al Aaraaf," is that its chain does not stop at the ceiling: it goes right on through the ceiling, through the roof, and up
to heaven. What comes down the chain from heaven is the divine
power of imagination, and it is imagination's purifying fire which
flashes or flickers from the chandelier. That is why the immaterial
and angelic Ligeia makes her reappearance directly beneath the
chandelier; and that is why Hop-Frog makes his departure for
dream-land by climbing the chandelier chain and vanishing through
the skylight.

The dreaming soul, then, has its own light—a light more spiritual,
more divine, than that of the sun. And Poe's chamber of dream is
autonomous in every other respect. No breath of air enters it from
the outside world: either its atmosphere is dead, or its draperies are
stirred by magical and intramural air currents. No earthly sound
invades the chamber: either it is deadly still, or it echoes with a
sourceless and unearthly music. Nor does any odor of flower or field
intrude: instead, as Poe tells in "The Assignation," the sense of smell
is "oppressed by mingled and conflicting perfumes, reeking up from
strange convolute censers."

The point of all this is that the dreaming psyche separates itself
wholly from the bodily senses—the "rudimental senses," as Poe
called them. The bodily senses are dependent on objective stimuli
—on the lights and sounds and odors of the physical world. But
the sensuous life of dream is self-sufficient and immaterial, and consists in the imagination's Godlike enjoyment of its own creations.

I am reminded, at this point, of a paragraph of Santayana's, in
which he describes the human soul as it was conceived by the philosopher Leibniz. Leibniz, says Santayana, assigned

a mental seat to all sensible objects. The soul, he said, had no windows and, he might have added, no doors; no light could come to it

from without; and it could not exert any transitive force or make any difference beyond its own insulated chamber. It was a *camera obscura*, with a universe painted on its impenetrable walls. The changes which went on in it were like those in a dream, due to the discharge of pent-up energies and fecundities within it . . .

Leibniz' chamber of the soul is identical with Poe's chamber of dream: but the solipsism which Leibniz saw as the normal human condition was for Poe an ideal state, a blessed state, which we may enjoy as children or as pre-existent souls, but can reclaim in adult life only by a flight from everyday consciousness into hypnagogic trance.

The one thing which remains to be said about Poe's buildings is that cellars or catacombs, whenever they appear, stand for the irrational part of the mind; and that is so conventional an equation in symbolic literature that I think I need not be persuasive or illustrative about it. I had hoped, at this point, to discuss in a leisurely way some of the stories in which Poe makes use of his architectural properties, treating those stories as narrative wholes. But I have spoken too long about other things; and so, if you will allow me a few minutes more, I shall close by commenting briskly on two or three stories only.

The typical Poe story occurs *within* the mind of a poet; and its characters are not independent personalities, but allegorical figures representing the warring principles of the poet's divided nature. The lady Ligeia, for example, stands for that heavenly beauty which the poet's soul desires; while Rowena stands for that earthly, physical beauty which tempts the poet's passions. The action of the story is the dreaming soul's gradual emancipation from earthly attachments—which is allegorically expressed in the slow dissolution of Rowena. The result of this process is the soul's final, momentary vision of the heavenly Ligeia. Poe's typical story presents some such struggle between the visionary and the mundane; and the duration of Poe's typical story is the duration of a dream.

There are two tales in which Poe makes an especially clear and simple use of his architectural symbolism. The first is an unfamiliar tale called "The System of Dr. Tarr and Prof. Fether," and the edifice of that tale is a remote and dilapidated madhouse in southern France. What happens, in brief, is that the inmates of the madhouse escape from their cells in the basement of the building, overpower their keepers, and lock them up in their own cells. Having done this, the lunatics take possession of the upper reaches of the house. They shutter all the windows, put on odd costumes, and proceed to hold an uproarious and discordant feast, during which there is much eating and drinking of a disgusting kind, and a degraded version of Ligeia or Helen does a strip tease. At the height of these festivities, the keepers escape from their cells, break in through the barred and shuttered windows of the dining room, and restore order.

Well: the madhouse, like all of Poe's houses, is a mind. The keepers are the rational part of that mind, and the inmates are its irrational part. As you noticed, the irrational is suitably assigned to the cellar. The uprising of the inmates, and the suppression of the keepers, symbolizes the beginning of a dream, and the mad banquet which follows is perhaps Poe's least spiritual portrayal of the dream state: *this* dream, far from being an escape from the physical, consists exclusively of the release of animal appetites—as dreams sometimes do. When the keepers break in the windows, and subdue the revellers, they bring with them reason and the light of day, and the wild dream is over.

"The Masque of the Red Death" is a better-known and even more obvious example of architectural allegory. You will recall how Prince Prospero, when his dominions are being ravaged by the plague, withdraws with a thousand of his knights and ladies into a secluded, impregnable and windowless abbey, where after a time he entertains his friends with a costume ball. The weird décor of the seven ballrooms expresses the Prince's own taste, and in strange costumes of the Prince's own design the company dances far into the night, looking, as Poe says, like "a multitude of dreams." The festivities are interrupted only by the hourly striking of a gigantic ebony clock which stands in the westernmost room; and the striking of this clock has invariably a sobering effect on the revellers. Upon the last stroke of twelve, as you will remember, there appears amid the throng a figure attired in the blood-dabbled graveclothes of a plague-victim. The dancers shrink from him in terror. But the Prince, infuriated at what he takes to be an insolent practical joke, draws his dagger and pursues the figure through all of the seven rooms. In the last and westernmost room, the figure suddenly turns and confronts Prince Prospero, who gives a cry of despair and falls upon his own dagger. The Prince's friends rush forward to seize the intruder, who stands now within the shadow of the ebony clock; but they find nothing there. And then, one after the other, the thousand revellers fall dead of the Red Death, and the lights flicker out, and Prince Prospero's ball is at an end.

In spite of its cast of one thousand and two, "The Masque of the Red Death" has only one character. Prince Prospero is one-half of that character, the visionary half; the nameless figure in graveclothes is the other, as we shall see in a moment.

More than once, in his dialogues or critical writings, Poe describes the earth-bound, time-bound rationalism of his age as a *disease*. And that is what the Red Death signifies. Prince Prospero's flight from the Red Death is the poetic imagination's flight from temporal and worldly consciousness into dream. The thousand dancers of Prince Prospero's costume ball are just what Poe says they are— "dreams" or "phantasms," veiled and vivid creatures of Prince Prospero's rapt imagination. Whenever there is a feast, or carnival, or costume ball in Poe, we may be sure that a dream is in progress.

But what is the gigantic ebony clock? For the answer to that, one need only consult a dictionary of slang: we call the human heart a *ticker,* meaning that it is the clock of the body; and that is what Poe means here. In sleep, our minds may roam beyond the temporal world, but our hearts tick on, binding us to time and mortality. Whenever the ebony clock strikes, the dancers of Prince Prospero's dream grow momentarily pale and still, in half-awareness that they and their revel must have an end; it is as if a sleeper should half-awaken, and know that he has been dreaming, and then sink back into dreams again.

The figure in blood-dabbled graveclothes, who stalks through the terrified company and vanishes in the shadow of the clock, is waking temporal consciousness, and his coming means the death of dreams. He breaks up Prince Prospero's ball as the keepers in "Dr. Tarr and Prof. Fether" break up the revels of the lunatics. The final confrontation between Prince Prospero and the shrouded figure is like the terrible final meeting between William Wilson and his double. Recognizing his adversary as his own worldly and mortal self, Prince Prospero gives a cry of despair which is also Poe's cry of despair: despair at the realization that only by self-destruction could the poet fully free his soul from the trammels of this world.

Poe's aesthetic, Poe's theory of the nature of art, seems to me insane. To say that art should repudiate everything human and earthly, and find its subject matter at the flickering end of dreams, is hopelessly to narrow the scope and function of art. Poe's aesthetic points toward such impoverishments as *poésie pure* and the abstract expressionist movement in painting. And yet, despite his aesthetic, Poe is a great artist, and I would rest my case for him on his prose allegories of psychic conflict. In them, Poe broke wholly new ground, and they remain the best things of their kind in our literature. Poe's mind may have been a strange one; yet all minds are alike in their general structure; therefore we can understand him, and I think that he will have something to say to us as long as there is civil war in the palaces of men's minds.

The Universe of Roderick Usher

by Maurice Beebe

To understand "The Fall of the House of Usher," it is necessary to know something of Poe's cosmology.[1] Although he did not sum up his philosophy until near the end of his life, when he wrote *Eureka,* Poe had long been attracted to philosophical and scientific works on the nature of the universe.[2] What the story of 1839 reveals through symbolic drama, the treatise of 1848 states through direct exposition; hence, an understanding of *Eureka* helps to clear up many of the ambiguities in a baffling story.

The universe, Poe says in *Eureka,* derives from a tiny particle of perfect oneness, matter in its utmost conceivable state of simplicity. From this initial unity are diffused spherically in all directions "a certain inexpressibly great yet limited number of unimaginably yet not infinitely minute atoms." [3] The agency of diffusion is radiation.

"The Universe of Roderick Usher," by Maurice Beebe. First published in slightly different form in *The Personalist,* XXXVII (Spring 1956) , 147-60. From *Ivory Towers and Sacred Founts: The Artist as Hero in Fiction from Goethe to Joyce.* © 1964 by New York University. Reprinted by permission of the author, *The Personalist,* and New York University Press.

[1] Allen Tate has said of Poe's symbols in general that they "refer to a known traditional of thought, an intelligible order, apart from what he was as a man, and are not merely the index to a compulsive neurosis." See "The Angelic Imagination: Poe as God," in his *The Forlorn Demon: Didactic and Critical Essays* (Chicago: Henry Regnery, 1953), pp. 59-60. In another essay, "Our Cousin, Mr. Poe," Tate analyzes "The Fall of the House of Usher" in relation to the vampire theme in Poe's fiction and, without developing the idea, states in passing that the catastrophe of the story illustrates the central thesis of *Eureka.* See *The Forlorn Demon,* pp. 86-89.

[2] Poe is presumably the author of a series of articles on the solar system published in *The Southern Literary Messenger* during 1838 which anticipate the ideas later elaborated in *Eureka.* See Margaret Alterton, *The Origins of Poe's Critical Theory, Iowa Humanistic Studies,* II, No. 3 (Iowa City, 1922), 144.

[3] *Eureka: An Essay on the Material and Spiritual Universe.* In *The Complete Works of Edgar Allan Poe,* ed. James A. Harrison (New York: Thomas Y. Crowell, 1902), XVI, 208.

The material-spiritual universe consists of tense relationships between the radiated particles—a continual struggle between attraction and repulsion, contraction and expansion. The law of gravity demonstrates the desire of all things to return to their initial unity. Against attraction or gravitation is the power of repulsion, or what Poe calls radiation. Since matter can be perceived only through its properties of attraction and repulsion and therefore *is* only attraction and repulsion, a finally consolidated, completely *attracted* universe would be a realm of no-matter or nothingness. The diffusing, radiating, repulsing agency, Poe believes, grows progressively weaker. When it can no longer withstand the power of attraction, all particles will return to oneness and the universe will disappear. The process of expansion and contraction may, however, be renewed again and again—"a novel Universe swelling into existence, and then subsiding into nothingness, at every throb of the Heart Divine." [4]

Poe equates the Heart Divine with the artist, and there is a close analogy between his cosmology and his theory of the short story. The artistic imagination is for Poe a creative power which disperses elements previously ordered by God and reassembles them into new unities or totalities. In his discussion of the short story, Poe says: "In the whole composition there should be no word written of which the tendency, direct or indirect, is not to the one pre-established design." [5] In *Eureka,* which was composed at about the same time as his theory of the short story, he says: "In the construction of *plot* . . . we should aim at so arranging the incidents that we shall not be able to determine, of any one of them, whether it depends from any one other or upholds it. In this sense, of course, *perfection* of *plot* is really, or practically, unattainable—but only because it is a finite intelligence that constructs. The plots of God are perfect. The Universe is a plot of God." [6]

The universe is the perfect plot of God because, since everything derives from the same basic oneness, each particle attracts each other particle. Cause is virtually indistinguishable from effect. If matter sprang from nothingness, it had to be created: a God exists to create a single particle which is the central core from which all other mat-

[4] *Eureka,* p. 208.
[5] *Selected Poetry and Prose,* p. 381.
[6] *Eureka,* p. 292.

ter is diffused. Yet, Poe implies elsewhere in *Eureka,* the agent is not really distinct from the substance: the things in the universe are "really but infinite individualizations of Himself";[7] and "God— the material *and* spiritual God—*now* exists solely in the diffused Matter and Spirit of the universe." [8] Thus cause becomes effect, and effect, cause.

Poe's use of the term "plot" to describe the creation of the universe is in agreement with his theory of the short story. The tale, Poe says, derives from a central core of *single effect* to which all elements must be related. The writer first determines the end of his story, the climax or catastrophe or solution which links and resolves all the earlier details. Then, working backward, he builds upon this central core increasingly diffuse, though always relevant, details. The writer's task is analogous to the cosmic process of expansion through radiation. The reader—who, Poe insists, must contemplate "with a kindred art"—begins at the level of greatest expansion and, linking detail to detail, reaches the climactic oneness which was, for the artist, the beginning of the story. The reader's task is analogous to the cosmic process of contraction through attraction.

The completed short story, like the completed universe, remains unified in that every element depends on the others. "Bear in mind," Poe says in the concluding sentence of *Eureka,* "that all is life—life —life within life, the less within the greater, and all within the Spirit Divine." From the initial unity of singleness comes the unity of mutual relationship. In the ideal short story, like the universe, everything is related and nothing is irrelevant. "The Fall of the House of Usher," many critics have found, is a nearly perfect illustration of Poe's theory of totality. That there are no collateral lines of the Usher family, that the name "House of Usher" signifies to its neighbors both the mansion and the family, that there is a barely perceptible crack running from roof to base of the house, that Roderick Usher has a particularly acute sense of hearing—all such details contribute to the single effect of the story and play a part in the final catastrophe.

The house of Usher is like the universe not only in that everything is related but also in that it is limited. In *Eureka* Poe insists

[7] *Ibid.,* p. 314.
[8] *Ibid.,* p. 313.

that the universe we know is not infinite and that there may be many neighboring universes each with its own god. As a result, our universe could conceivably be entered and left again. The same is true of the house of Usher, and Poe permits us to crack the shell with the narrator, who comes from outside, travels the "whole of a . . . day" through "a singularly dreary tract of country," arrives at "an atmosphere which had no affinity with the air of heaven," enters the house, walks "through many dark and intricate passages," meets Roderick Usher in what appears to be the central apartment, is a reluctant observer of all that occurs, and finally leaves—a rounded process which in itself suggests the circle-like unity of the story. The emphasis on the isolation of the house of Usher helps the impression of a self-contained world, a totality.

Within the unity of the house of Usher are many diffusions in the form of mirrored or echo-like correspondences. The house is reflected in the tarn. Roderick and Madeline are twins between whom "sympathies of a scarcely intelligible nature" had always existed. Roderick's painting suggests Madeline's vault. The sounds described in "Mad Trist" are echoed by the noises which accompany Madeline as she seeks her revenge. The storm outside the window reflects the storm within Roderick's mind. His song, "The Haunted Palace," relates symbolically the union between the "radiant palace" and the mind of its tenant, and—a key element in the structural unity—it is Poe's story in capsule form.

The main line of diffusion runs chainlike from the tarn to the house to Roderick to Madeline. The narrator, arriving before the "mansion of gloom," is immediately conscious of the isolated and self-contained atmosphere of the place:

> It was possible, I reflected, that a mere different arrangement of the particulars of the scene, of the details of the picture, would be sufficient to modify, or perhaps to annihilate its capacity for sorrowful impression; and, acting upon this idea, I reined my horse to the precipitous brink of a black and lurid tarn that lay in unruffled lustre by the dwelling, and gazed down—but with a shudder even more thrilling than before—upon the remodelled and inverted image of the gray sedge, and the ghastly tree-stems, and the vacant and eye-like windows.

One feature of the house is the "barely perceptible fissure, which extending from the roof of the building in front, made its way down the wall in a zigzag direction, until it became lost in the sullen waters of the tarn." The "unruffled" tarn may be interpreted as the oneness or nothingness from which all has emerged and to which all must return.

The next link of diffusion is the correspondence between the house of Usher and Roderick. In addition to several analogies described in "The Haunted Palace," many details in the story express the relationship. The "eye-like windows" and doors like "ponderous and ebony jaws" are the most obvious. The "minute *fungi* . . . hanging in a fine tangled web-work from the eaves" is equivalent to Roderick Usher's hair "of a more than weblike softness and tenuity." The "wild inconsistency" between the house's "perfect adaptation of parts, and the crumbling condition of the individual stones" is the "inconsistency" which arises from Roderick's "feeble and futile struggle to overcome an habitual trepidancy." The crack in the building corresponds to Roderick's struggle against insanity, his effort to maintain his composure against what may be called the "kingdom of inorganization."

The fissure in the building also corresponds to the diffusion split between Roderick and Madeline. Just as the house and Roderick are included within the range and influence of the tarn, the house is equal to both the Ushers. In a sense, however, Madeline is subordinate to her brother. Poe tells us that there had always been an "undeviating transmission, from sire to son, of the patrimony with the name." This would imply that there has been but one surviving male Usher in each generation and that the daughters, who need not have appeared in every generation, have either failed to marry or to survive. The "sympathies of a scarcely intelligible nature" between the twins would suggest that, like the two William Wilsons, the one must always suffer with the other. But, as far as most of Poe's narrative is concerned, it is Roderick who affects, Madeline who is affected. Her mysterious illness appears to be the reflection of his mental affliction. The relation between brother and sister is not unlike that of Dumas's Corsican brothers, one of whom responds to the other's actions and emotions. In Poe's story this is true only along the line of expansion; when the contraction begins, the relationship is reversed.

In the story, as in *Eureka,* the force of diffusion is radiation. Roderick Usher

> was enchained by certain superstitious impressions in regard to the dwelling which he tenanted, and whence, for many years, he had never ventured forth—in regard to an influence whose supposititious force was conveyed in terms too shadowy here to be re-stated—an influence which some peculiarities in the mere form and substance of his family mansion, had, by dint of long sufferance, he said, obtained over his spirit—an effect which the *physique* of the grey walls and turrets, and of the dim tarn into which they all looked down, had, at length, brought about upon the *morale* of his existence.

The power of the mansion and the tarn to influence the mind of Roderick is, in part, explained by his belief in the sentience of things. The narrator scoffs at this "superstition," but lists in a footnote four authorities for the idea. It was not so much the novelty of animism as the "pertinacity" with which Roderick Usher held the conviction that made it important: "in his disordered fancy, the idea had assumed a more daring character, and trespassed, under certain conditions, upon the kingdom of inorganization." Evidence of this sentience Roderick found in "the gradual yet certain condensation of an atmosphere of their own about the waters and walls." The narrator, too, has noticed the "pestilent and mystic vapour, dull, sluggish, faintly discernible, and leaden-hued" which apparently "had reeked up from the decayed trees, and the grey wall, and the silent tarn." "An atmosphere of their own" suggests that the house and its domains have not only sentience but also the power to transmit it—that is, to radiate.

Poe's own philosophy was as animistic as Roderick Usher's. Throughout *Eureka* he makes no distinction between vegetable or biological life and inanimate matter. Matter, he says, is but attraction and repulsion: "The former is the Body; the latter the Soul: the one is the material; the other the spiritual, principle of the Universe. *No other principles exist.*" [9] And "thus the two Principles Proper, *Attraction* and *Repulsion*—the material and the spiritual —accompany each other, in the strictest fellowship, forever. Thus

[9] *Ibid.,* pp. 213-14.

The Body and The Soul walk hand in hand." [10] The Divine Being, Poe says,

> now feels his life through an infinity of imperfect pleasures—the partial and pain-intertangled pleasures of those inconceivably numerous things which you designate as his creatures, but which are really but infinite individualizations of Himself. All these creatures—*all*—those which you term animate, as well as those to whom you deny life for no better reason than that you do not behold it in operation —*all* these creatures have, in greater or less degree, a capacity for pleasure and for pain. . . . These creatures are all too, more or less conscious Intelligences.[11]

A belief in the sentience of things is a necessary corollary of Poe's insistence on unity. Because the heart divine is "our own," each soul "is, in part, its own God—its own Creator." [12]

Poe's equating of agent with substance permits us to understand how Roderick Usher, presumably a created being, can influence his environment as well as be affected by it. While his *morale* is affected by the *physique* of his surroundings, his own mind helps to determine the character of the house and tarn. Roderick Usher is the dramatic center of the story, and we must see the chain from his point of view. When the narrator arrives before the house of Usher, "a sense of insufferable gloom" pervades his spirit. When he enters Roderick's studio, "an air of stern, deep, and irredeemable gloom hung over and pervaded all." The mystery of this recurrently mentioned gloom is solved when the narrator perceives "the futility of all attempt at cheering a mind from which darkness, as if an inherent positive quality, poured forth upon all objects of the moral and physical universe, in *one unceasing radiation of gloom.*"

Roderick's power to radiate is intensified by his art. We have seen that if the universe is a plot of God, a story resembles the universe and the artist resembles God. The peculiarity of the Usher family is "a passionate devotion to the intricacies, perhaps even more than to the orthodox and easily recognizable beauties, of musical science." Music is the most appropriate art for the Ushers because waves of sound, particularly from stringed instruments, suggest the process of radiation. "The Haunted Palace," a sample of Roderick's musical

[10] *Ibid.*, p. 244.
[11] *Ibid.*, p. 314.
[12] *Ibid.*, p. 313.

gift, is sung to the accompaniment of a guitar, and the song itself is significant because it expresses Roderick's awareness of his own dilemma. He is also a painter. One of his pictures is described in detail:

> A small picture presented the interior of an immensely long and rectangular vault or tunnel, with low walls, smooth, white, and without interruption or device. Certain accessory points of the design served well to convey the idea that this excavation lay at an exceeding depth below the surface of the earth. No outlet was observed in any portion of its vast extent, and no torch, or other artificial source of light, was discernible; yet a flood of intense rays rolled throughout, and bathed the whole in a ghastly and inappropriate splendour.

We are told just before this description that "if ever mortal painted an idea, that mortal was Roderick Usher," and of his paintings that "an excited and highly distempered ideality threw a sulphureous lustre over all." As one of the many mirror-like diffusions in the story, the picture represents Madeline's vault. (On a different level, it is Poe's short story.) The fact that there is no visible outlet suggests a totality, and the "flood of intense rays" implies the "sulphureous lustre" that radiates from Roderick's (or Poe's) mind.

Roderick's artistic activities are closely related to his sanity. It is significant that after Madeline has been buried, "his ordinary occupations were neglected or forgotten." As long as Roderick continues the diffusive power symbolized by his music and his painting, he can maintain the delicate balance between repulsion and attraction and save himself from annihilation. Yet, it is his awareness of his tense situation that finally drives him mad. The first step toward insanity is his acceptance of animism and his sense of intimate relationship with the objects about him. Any movement, Poe says in *Eureka,* sets off a chain reaction that affects every part of the whole:

> If I venture to displace, by even the billionth part of an inch, the microscopial speck of dust which lies now upon the point of my finger, what is the character of that act upon which I have adventured? I have done a deed which shakes the Moon in her path, which causes the Sun to be no longer the Sun, and which alters forever the destiny of the multitudinous myriads of stars that roll and glow in the majestic presence of their Creator.[13]

[13] *Ibid.,* p. 218.

It is not difficult to see that such a belief could lead to a morbid sensitivity. Roderick

> suffered much from a morbid acuteness of the senses; the most insipid food was alone endurable; he could wear only garments of a certain texture; the odours of all flowers were oppressive; his eyes were tortured by even a faint light; and there were but peculiar sounds, and these from stringed instruments, which did not inspire him with horror.

Some years after the story was first published, Poe added as a motto the appropriate heart-lute image from De Béranger:

> Son cœur est un luth suspendu,
> Sitôt qu'on le touche il résonne.

As used here, the lute is an intermediary. While Roderick maintains the balance between reception and transmission, he is sane. When he only receives, he becomes a passive prey to the "kingdom of inorganization." In "The Haunted Palace," built on contrasting images of reason-order and madness-disorder,

> Spirits moving musically
> To a lute's well-tuned law

become

> Vast forms that move fantastically
> To a discordant melody.[14]

The problem of motivation has perplexed many critics of "The Fall of the House of Usher." To the extent that Roderick's actions may be attributed to insanity, the question of motivation is beside the point. And, at any rate, whether or not Roderick wills his fate is less important than that the fate does occur. In line with *Eureka,* however, Roderick Usher is both the agent of his fate and its object. There is sufficient internal evidence in the tale to suggest that Roderick deliberately buried his sister alive. He paints the picture of Madeline's vault before he places her there. Poe emphasizes the screwing down of the coffin lid. After the burial, "there were times, indeed," says the narrator, "when I thought his unceasingly agitated

[14] A more complete discussion of the reason-order and madness-disorder symbols is to be found in Darrel Abel, "A Key to the House of Usher," *University of Toronto Quarterly,* XVIII (January 1949), 176-85.

mind was labouring with some oppressive secret, to divulge which
he struggled for the necessary courage." He would have known that
while he lives, Madeline is not dead. When, in the climax of the
story, he hears her approaching, he cries, "Is she not hurrying to
upbraid me for my haste?" And, certainly, there is every appearance
of vengeance about Madeline when she appears at the door of the
room. Madeline is Roderick's "tenderly beloved sister," but his realization that her terrible illness is the product of his mental affliction
leads him to what could be described as a mercy killing—and a
suicide.

Roderick's motivation may be explained in terms of *Eureka*. The
general proposition of Poe's treatise is: *"In the Original Unity of
the First Thing lies the Secondary Cause of All Things, with the
Germ of their Inevitable Annihilation."* [15] Once diffused, every particle desires to return to the initial singleness: "A diffusion from
unity," Poe says, "involves a tendency to return into unity—a tendency ineradicable until satisfied." [16] Inevitably, the diffusing agency
becomes weakened. Roderick is apparently a deterioration of his
ancestors, and the presence of the narrator implies that Roderick
was stronger in the past than in the present. When he can no longer
stand to be a tense, suffering creature, attracting and repulsing, attracted and repulsed, he seeks a return to the unity of no-attraction-
repulsion, no-matter, nothingness. He is like Ethelred, the hero of
"Mad Trist," who, "having sought in vain for peaceable admission
into the dwelling of the hermit [aloneness, oneness], proceeds to
make good an entrance by force." By burying his sister alive, Roderick tries to halt the diffusion. The totality symbolically presented
in his picture of Madeline's vault implies, in a sense, the comple-
tion of expansion, the attempt to become independent of the diffused portion of himself by isolating it. The Divine Being, Poe
says in *Eureka*, "passes His eternity in perpetual variation of Concentrated Self and almost infinite Self-Diffusion." [17] Godlike Roderick's action is the peak of the self-diffusion, the beginning of a
return to a concentrated oneness, which, as we have seen, is nothingness and annihilation. After Madeline is placed in the tomb,

[15] *Eureka*, pp. 185-86.
[16] *Ibid.*, p. 207.
[17] *Ibid.*, p. 314.

Roderick's "ordinary manner had vanished . . . the luminousness of his eye had utterly gone out."

We can better understand Roderick's motivation if we recognize its parallel in Poe's life. Many students of Poe have considered him a virtual suicide. A few months before his death he wrote to Mrs. Clemm: "It is no use to reason with me *now;* I must die. I have no desire to live since I have done 'Eureka.' I could accomplish nothing more." [18] His almost triumphant despair is expressed in the conclusion of his treatise. Every creature, person, and thing, he says, is a conscious intelligence—"conscious, first, of a proper identity; conscious, secondly, and by faint indeterminate glimpses, of an identity with the Divine Being of whom we speak—of an identity with God." [19] The first consciousness, Poe says, will grow weaker as the latter becomes stronger, and when the sense of individual identity has been merged in the general consciousness, man "will at length attain that awfully triumphant epoch when he shall recognize his existence as that of Jehovah." [20] Shortly before this prediction appears a revealing passage:

> In this view, and in this view alone, we comprehend the riddles of Divine Injustice—of Inexorable Fate. In this view alone the existence of Evil becomes intelligible; but in this view it becomes more—it becomes endurable. Our souls no longer rebel at a *Sorrow* which we ourselves have imposed upon ourselves, in furtherance of our own purposes—with a view—if even with a futile view—to the extension of our Joy.[21]

The evil "sorrow" refers, I assume, to Poe's self-imposed tortures, particularly his drinking and drug-taking. He now recognizes such activity as a projection from the self, a form of diffusion not unlike the creating of art. No longer rebelling at the sorrow which accompanies it, he solaces himself with the conviction that such activity, carried to its furthest extent, may annihilate an identity that has become repugnant to him. Like Roderick Usher, he seeks a return to *oneness.* Before the burial, Roderick's voice had "that leaden,

[18] *The Letters of Edgar Allan Poe,* ed. John Ward Ostrom (Cambridge, Mass.: Harvard University Press, 1948), II, 452.
[19] *Eureka,* p. 314.
[20] *Ibid.,* p. 315.
[21] *Ibid.,* p. 313.

self-balanced and perfectly modulated guttural utterance, which may be observed in the lost drunkard, or the irreclaimable eater of opium, during the period of his most intense excitement." After the burial, "the once occasional huskiness of his voice was heard no more." No longer self-balanced, the diffusion has been carried to the point of annihilation.

Although the radiation from Roderick's consciousness ceases with the burying of his sister, the diffused particles remain and begin their return. They must now return because there is nothing to hold them back. The "gradual yet certain condensation of an atmosphere of their own about the waters and walls" becomes, in the climactic scene, "the unnatural light of a faintly luminous and distinctly visible gaseous exhalation which hung about and enshrouded the mansion." The narrator says, "The exceeding density of the clouds (which hung so low as to press upon the turrets of the house) did not prevent our perceiving the lifelike velocity with which they flew careering from all points against each other, without passing away into the distance." The narrator, trying to comfort his disturbed friend, unwittingly tells him a truth that could well increase the terror: " 'These appearances, which bewilder you, are merely electrical phenomena not uncommon—or it may be that they have their ghastly origin in the rank miasma of the tarn.' "

Roderick is linked as closely in one direction to his sister as, in the other direction, to the house and the tarn. And, of course, Madeline must return upon him also. The supernatural—the lid of the coffin was screwed down—has a philosophical, if not a natural, explanation. When the movement reaches the end of the chain of expansion, it must return along the line of contraction. Roderick, who formerly acted upon his sister, has now become the passive victim. With the destruction of the part occurs the annihilation of the whole.

The house should be destroyed simultaneously with the death of the last of the Ushers, but Poe has to let the narrator escape to tell his story. As a result, the last paragraph not only concludes the tale but also repeats, in concentrated form, the unity-radiation-diffusion-return-to-unity process which has determined the ideological structure of the story. In a marginal revision of *Eureka* Poe said of a passage on the act of diffusion, "Here describe the process as one instantaneous flash." [22] The House of Usher splits first into two parts, corresponding to the many delicately balanced diffusion-correspondences in the story. The crack widens, suggesting Roderick's insanity, his inability to maintain balance, and hence his desperate effort to become independent of the diffused matter. The two parts split into many fragments as the peak of diffusion occurs. The last sentence suggests a return to the original unity: "My brain reeled as I saw the mighty walls rushing asunder—there was a long tumultuous shouting like the voice of a thousand waters—and the deep and dank tarn at my feet closed suddenly and silently over the fragments of the 'House of Usher.' "

Many of Poe's stories demonstrate his strictures on the unity of single effect, but if my analysis of "The Fall of the House of Usher" is valid, it follows that the complete relevance of details in this story—a fact long acknowledged by critics—is not simply a matter of careful plotting in terms of a theory of aesthetic unity. Because the literary theory behind the story is actually religious in essence and because here content and form are one, we find in Roderick Usher an ideal and complete prototype of the artist-as-God. Roderick is not depicted as a person in the universe; he is himself his universe. The power to create is the power to destroy, and his most triumphant creation is the obliteration of his suffering, diffused self in a return to that oneness which is nothingness. His French followers also sought to create themselves, and some of them at least realized that to do so would mean annihilation of self in *le néant*.

[22] *Ibid.*, p. 326.

Meaning and
"The Masque of the Red Death"

by Joseph Patrick Roppolo

Those who seek guidance in interpreting Edgar Allan Poe's "The Masque of the Red Death" are doomed to enter a strange world, as confused and confusing as a Gothic Wonderland and in some respects as eerie as the blighted house of Roderick Usher. Their guides will be old critics, New Critics, scholars, biographers, enthusiasts, dilettantes, journalists, hobbyists, anthologists, medical men, psychologists, and psychoanalysts. From these the seekers will learn that Prince Prospero is Poe himself and that "The Masque" is therefore autobiography; that Poe never presents a moral; that "The Masque" is an allegory and must therefore teach a lesson; that there is indeed a moral; that there are unnumbered morals; that there is no message or meaning; that there is a message; that the message is quite obvious and understandable; and that the meaning of the message transcends human understanding. In the pages that follow I should like to tour, briefly, the tangled world of the critics of "The Masque of the Red Death" and then to explore "The Masque" with the best of all possible guides—Poe himself.

I

A representative of the psychological guide and of the group which sees no meaning in "The Masque of the Red Death" is Albert Mordell, whose book, *The Erotic Motive in Literature,* widely read since 1919, was reissued in 1962 with a new section on Poe.

"Meaning and 'The Masque of the Red Death,'" by Joseph Patrick Roppolo. From *Tulane Studies in English,* XIII (1963), 59-69. © 1964 by Tulane University. Reprinted by permission of the author.

Mordell writes blithely of Poe's "Loss of Breadth" and of a character named Roger Usher who, "like Poe, had been disappointed in love, and probably also drank." [1] To Mordell, Poe was not only a frustrated lover and a drunkard; he was also a sadist and a masochist, a man who suffered from "a damming of the libido" and who was "so absorbed in his dreams that he never tried to take an interest in reality. Hence," Mordell concludes, "we will find no moral note in Poe's work"—with the single exception of "William Wilson." [2]

In sharp contrast, Vincent Buranelli argues that Poe "was no sadist, no masochist, no pervert, no rake," but was instead "the sanest of our writers"—that he was, in fact, "America's greatest writer, and the American writer of greatest significance in world literature." [3] Yet, oddly, Buranelli finds himself aligned with Mordell when he, too, asserts sweepingly that "Poe does not touch morality"; and he finds himself involved in something of a contradiction when he describes "The Masque of the Red Death" as "an allegory representing Death itself as one of the *dramatis personae*." [4] Allegory, typically, is meaningful and moral, but Buranelli does not elaborate upon his statement; nor does he reconcile Poe's well-known detestation of allegory with Poe's use of it in one of his acknowledged masterpieces.[5]

Joseph Wood Krutch, who saw Poe as incompetent, sexless, and mad, but nevertheless marked by genius, dismissed "The Masque of the Red Death" as "merely the most perfect [*sic*] description of that fantastic *décor* which [Poe] had again and again imagined." [6] Edward H. Davidson remarks on the paucity of "fact and information" in the piece and reveals that "tone and movement are all." [7] Commenting at greater length, David M. Rein summarizes the narrative and adds that

---

[1] See Albert Mordell, *The Erotic Motive in Literature* (New York: Collier Books, 1962), pp. 173-75. Apparently Mordell was unaware of his remarkable Freudian slip in renaming Roderick Usher. The reference to "Loss of Breath" occurs on p. xxi. It is, perhaps (hopefully), a printer's error.

[2] *Ibid.*, pp. 174, 175, and (especially) 177.

[3] Vincent Buranelli, *Edgar Allan Poe* (New York: Twayne Publishers, Inc., 1961), pp. 44, 63, and 133.

[4] *Ibid.*, pp. 72, 73.

[5] Buranelli himself (p. 125) refers to the fact that Poe "detested . . . allegory."

[6] Joseph Wood Krutch, *Edgar Allan Poe: A Study in Genius* (New York: Alfred A. Knopf, 1926), p. 77.

[7] Edward H. Davidson, *Poe: A Critical Study* (Cambridge: The Belknap Press of Harvard University Press, 1957), p. 154.

The prince, of course, represents Poe, once again as a young man of wealthy and distinguished family. Here Poe dreamed of escape from the harsh world, where such evils as the plague were dominant —escape into a secluded place of pleasure he himself designed. But like so many of Poe's fantasies, this dream world would not remain intact; the imaginary refuge, in spite of all precautions, was invaded by Death, whose merest look destroyed him. It may be significant, too, that all in this company fell back to avoid encountering the gruesome figure. The prince alone, unwilling to await the stranger's pleasure, went forth to pursue him. Does not Poe here once again, in fantasy, impatiently seek a danger that seems inescapable? [8]

Avoiding the pitfall of imagining Poe's ratiocinative mind losing control of a carefully imagined dream world, Killis Campbell, among others, contented himself with seeking sources and with attempting to ground the fantasy of "The Masque of the Red Death" in fact. In *The Mind of Poe and Other Studies,*[9] Campbell points out that Poe was "pretty clearly indebted to William Harrison Ainsworth's *Old Saint Paul's*" and then cites an account by N. P. Willis in the *New York Mirror* of June 2, 1832, in which Willis describes a Parisian ball featuring "The Cholera Waltz," "The Cholera Galopade," and, most pertinently, a masked figure representing the cholera itself. Willard Thorp, in *A Southern Reader,*[10] makes the identity of Poe's Red Death positive: it is, Thorp says, "undoubtedly the cholera, newly arrived in America"; Poe colors it red to distinguish it from the Black Death—the bubonic plague.[11] In a more literary vein, numerous scholars have pointed out the use of the words "red plague" by Shakespeare in *The Tempest* (I,ii,364), without, however, making useful applications to Poe's "Masque."

Arthur Hobson Quinn is among those who believe that "The Masque of the Red Death" contains a moral or a message (he uses the terms interchangeably). "With a restraint that is one of the surest marks of genius," Quinn says, "Poe gives no hint of the great moral the tale tells to those who can think. For the others, he had

[8] David M. Rein, *Edgar A. Poe: The Inner Pattern* (New York: Philosophical Library. 1960), p. 33.
[9] Cambridge, Mass.: Harvard University Press, 1933. See p. 177 and note.
[10] New York: Alfred A. Knopf, 1955. See p. 656n.
[11] To my knowledge no one has pointed out that cholera generally—both in the popular mind and etymologically—has been and is associated with yellow.

no message." [12] Whereupon Quinn leaves his reader to place himself among the thinkers or, unhappily, among the non-thinkers, disdaining to make explicit or even to suggest the "great moral" which Poe shields behind his "Masque."

Patrick F. Quinn agrees that "The Masque of the Red Death" is "one of the few serious moral tales that Poe ever wrote," [13] but he, too, spares the reader the embarrassment of having the moral or morals pointed out to him. Others are less reticent, and their interpretations tend to fall into the familiar pattern of the *memento mori*. Typical are Frances Winwar and Norman Foerster.

To Frances Winwar, "The Masque of the Red Death" is "a compelling fantasy in scarlet and black where every effect stresses the inevitability of final dissolution. . . ." [14] Foerster notes that red is "Poe's most frequent color" and sees in it "the horror of blood." To Foerster "The Masque of the Red Death" is a richly vivid contrast between life and death. Setting dominates, and "magnificence and voluptuousness heighten the sense of worldly pleasure till the heart of life beats feverishly—and stops." The clock symbolizes the processes of time—both life and death.[15]

Three critics, Walter Blair, Harry Levin, and Marie Bonaparte, go far beyond the routine. To Blair, as to many others, there is "allegorical signification" in the seven rooms, which, "progressing from east to west—from blue to black—connote the seven ages of man from the blue of the dawn of life to the black of its night." The clock is, of course, Time; the masked figure is the Red Death; and the revelers are the living, "who seek to bar out and forget death by being gay and carefree," only to discover that death must inevitably conquer all humanity. So far, the critic is in the mainstream of interpretation. But Blair, more perceptive than most, refuses to confine "The Masque of the Red Death" to this moral. The closing note of the last paragraph is "inconsistent with such a meaning"; and Poe, a lover of ambiguity, would probably argue, Blair says, that

[12] Arthur Hobson Quinn, *Edgar Allan Poe: A Critical Biography* (New York: D. Appleton-Century Company, Inc., 1941), p. 331.

[13] Patrick F. Quinn, *The French Face of Edgar Allan Poe* (Carbondale: Southern Illinois University Press, 1957), p. 115.

[14] Frances Winwar, *The Haunted Palace: A Life of Edgar Allan Poe* (New York: Harper & Brothers, Publishers, 1959), p. 227.

[15] Norman Foerster, ed., *American Poetry and Prose* (Boston: Houghton Mifflin Company, 1957), I, 424.

"The Masque" is "suggestive of implications which cannot be made explicit this side of eternity." [16] Harry Levin makes the venture. "The closing note, echoed from the pseudo-Miltonic last line of Pope's *Dunciad*," Levin says, "predicates a reduction of cosmos to chaos" [17]—a challenging and, I hope to show, a fruitful bit of speculation.

It is left to Princess Bonaparte to lift "The Masque of the Red Death" from the limited realm of allegory to the expansive kingdom of myth. But, having placed "The Masque" among "typical" Oedipus stories, along with "The Cask of Amontillado," the Princess bogs down in a morass of conflicting Freudian symbols. The Prince, of course, is Oedipus, the son. The masked figure is the father. The castle of seven rooms is the body of the mother. The uplifted dagger is a phallus. The dropped dagger is the castrated phallus. And the Red Death—whether father-figure or something beyond that—is both death and castration.[18] We are back in the weird and wonderful world of Albert Mordell, who, not surprisingly, admits owing a great debt to Princess Bonaparte.

Of all the critics mentioned, Blair is the most detailed and in many ways the most convincing. Foerster's brief statement, too, almost compels belief. But I should like to suggest that neither goes far enough. Foerster evades consideration of Poe's final paragraph. Blair acknowledges that paragraph—vitally important because of its position—but leaves all attempts at its clarification to the other side of eternity. If Foerster's evasion is justified (and Levin's remark indicates that it is not), then Poe has failed to follow one of his own precepts, that "In the whole composition there should be no word written, of which the tendency, direct or indirect, is not to be the one pre-established design." [19] And if Blair is correct, then Poe must have sprinkled his page with more than a grain of salt when he wrote that "Every work of art should contain within itself all that

---

[16] Walter Blair, "Poe's Conception of Incident and Tone in the Tale," *Modern Philology*, XLI (May 1944), 228-40, especially pp. 239, 240.

[17] Harry Levin, *The Power of Blackness: Hawthorne, Poe, Melville* (New York: Vintage Books, 1960), p. 150.

[18] Marie Bonaparte, *The Life and Works of Edgar Allan Poe: A Psychoanalytic Approach* (London: Imago Publishing Co., Ltd., 1949), pp. 513, 515. Princess Bonaparte's conclusion is interesting: for Prospero, "as for Poe," she says, ". . . sensual delight had no genital expression."

[19] In Poe's "Review of Nathaniel Hawthorne's *Twice-Told Tales*."

is requisite for its own comprehension." [20] I do not believe that Poe was less than a remarkably skilled craftsman, nor do I believe that his critical dicta were deliberate jests. I should like to take Poe at his word in both quoted statements and, with both steadily in mind, study "The Masque of the Red Death" to see what it yields.

II

In Poe's imaginative prose, beginnings unfailingly are important. "The Masque of the Red Death" begins with these three short sentences:

> The "Red Death" had long devastated the country. No pestilence had even been so fatal or so hideous. Blood was its Avatar and its seal—the redness and horror of blood.

On one level, the reader is introduced to a disease, a plague, with hideous and terrifying symptoms, a remarkably rapid course, and inevitable termination in death. But Poe's heaviest emphasis is on blood, not as sign or symptom, but as avatar and seal. A seal is something that confirms or assures or ratifies. The appearance— the presence—of blood is confirmation or assurance of the existence of the Red Death or, more broadly, of Death itself. As avatar, blood is the incarnation, the bodily representation, of the Red Death. It is, further, something godlike, an eternal principle, for in Hindu myth, the word "avatar" referred to the descent of a god, in human form, to earth. Further, "avatar" can be defined as "a variant phase or version of a continuing entity." [21] A second level thus emerges: blood represents something invisible and eternal, a ruling principle of the universe. That principle, Poe seems to suggest, is death.

But is it? The Red Death, Poe tells us, "had long devastated the country." And then: "No pestilence had ever been so fatal"—surely a remarkable second sentence for a man so careful of grammar and logic as Poe. Is or is not the Red Death a pestilence? And does the word "fatal" permit of comparison? I should like to suggest that here Poe is being neither ungrammatical nor even carefully ambiguous, but daringly clear. The Red Death is not a pestilence, in the

---

[20] In Poe's essay, "Longfellow's Ballads."

[21] Reference to the *OED* will show that all meanings given here for *seal* and *avatar* were current in Poe's time.

usual sense; it is unfailingly and universally fatal, as no mere disease or plague can be; and blood is its guarantee, its avatar and seal. Life itself, then, is the Red Death, the one "affliction" shared by all mankind.[22]

For purposes of commenting on life and of achieving his single effect, Poe chooses to emphasize death. He is aware not only of the brevity of all life and of its inevitable termination but also of men's isolation: blood, the visible sign of life, is, Poe says, "the pest ban which shuts him out from the aid and sympathy of his fellow man." In the trap of life and in his death, every man *is* an island. If there is a mutual bond, it is the shared horror of death.

Out of the chaos that has "long devastated" his dominions, Prince Prospero creates a new and smaller world for the preservation of life. A kind of demigod, Prospero can "create" his world, and he can people it; but time (the ebony clock) exists in his new world, and he is, of course, deluded in his belief that he can let in life and shut out death. Prospero's world of seven rooms, without "means [either] of ingress or egress," is a microcosm, as the parallel with the seven ages of man indicates, and its people are eminently human, with their predilection for pleasure and their susceptibility to "sudden impulses of despair or frenzy." In their masquerade costumes, the people are "in fact, a multitude of dreams," but they are fashioned like the inhabitants of the macrocosmic world. Many are beautiful, but many also are bizarre or grotesque. Some are wanton; some are "arabesque figures with unsuited limbs and appointments"; some are terrible, some are disgusting, and some are "delirious fancies such as the madman fashions" (and Prospero, the demigod, for all his "fine eye for colors and effects," may indeed be mad). But all of them are life, and in six of the seven apartments "the heart of life" beats "feverishly." And even here, by deliberate use of the word "feverishly," Poe links life with disease and death.

The seventh apartment is not the room of death; death occurs in fact in each of the rooms. It is, however, the room in which the

---

[22] For the life of all flesh is the blood thereof" (*Leviticus*, 17:14). Poe knew the Bible well, and references to and quotations from the Bible are frequent in his works. In *Biblical Allusions in Poe* (New York: The Macmillan Company, 1928), William Mentzel Forrest says that Poe's views on death are "essentially Biblical" and points out that "Throughout the Old Testament death is looked upon not from the religious but from the natural viewpoint, as something to which all life is subject in harmony with the great laws of change" (p. 58).

reminders of death are strongest, and it is the room to which all must come who traverse the preceding six. Death's colors, red and black, are there; and there the ebony clock mercilessly measures Time, reminding the revelers hour after hour that life, like the course of the Red Death, is short.

When the clock strikes the dreaded hour of twelve, the revelers become aware suddenly of the presence of a masked figure which none has noted before:

> The figure was tall and gaunt, and shrouded from head to foot in the habiliments of the grave. The mask which concealed the visage was made so nearly to resemble the countenance of a stiffened corpse that the closest scrutiny must have had difficulty in detecting the cheat. And yet all this might have been endured, if not approved, by the mad revellers around. But the mummer had gone so far as to assume the type of the Red Death. His vesture was dabbled in *blood*— and his broad brow, with all the features of the face, was besprinkled with the scarlet horror.

Poe does not indicate in which room the awareness of the masked figure occurred first, but Prince Prospero sees this blood-sprinkled horror in the blue, or easternmost, room, which is usually associated with birth, rather than with death. The figure moves then through each of the apartments, and Prospero follows, to meet his own death in the room of black and red.

Not once does Poe say that the figure is the Red Death. Instead, "this new presence" is called "the masked figure," "the stranger," "the mummer," "this spectral image," and "the intruder." He is "shrouded" in "the habiliments of the grave," the dress provided by the living for their dead and endowed by the living with all the horror and terror which they associate with death. The mask, fashioned to resemble "the countenance of a stiffened corpse," is but a mask, a "cheat." And all this, we are told, "might have been borne" had it not been for the blood, that inescapable reminder to life of the inevitability of death. The intruder is, literally, "The *Mask* of the Red Death," [23] not the plague itself, nor even—as many would have it—the all-inclusive representation of Death.

There is horror in the discovery that "the grave-cerements and

[23] Poe's original title for this short prose piece, when it appeared in *Graham's Lady and Gentleman's Magazine* in May 1842, was "The Mask of the Red Death. A Fantasy."

corpse-like mask" are "untenanted by any tangible form," but the
horror runs more deeply than the supernatural interpretation allows, so deeply in fact that it washes itself clean to emerge as Truth.
Blood, Poe has been saying, is (or is symbolic of) the life force; but
even as it suggests life, blood serves as a reminder of death.[24] Man
himself invests death with elements of terror, and he clothes not
death but the terror of death in garb of his own making—"the
habiliments of the grave"—and then runs, foolishly, to escape it or,
madly, to kill it, mistaking the mummer, the cheat, for death itself.
The fear of death can kill: Prospero attempts to attack the masked
figure and falls; but when man's image of death is confronted directly, it is found to be nothing. The vestments are empty. The
intruder in "The Masque of the Red Death" is, then, not the plague,
not death itself, but man's creation, his self-aroused and self-devel-
oped fear of his own mistaken concept of death.

Death is nevertheless present, as pervasive and as invisible as
eternal law. He is nowhere and everywhere, not only near, about,
and around man, but in him. And so it is, at last, that, having un-
masked their unreasoning fear, the revelers acknowledge the presence of the Red Death. One by one, the revelers die—as everything
endowed with life must; and, with the last of them, time, which is
measured and feared only by man, dies, too.[25]

Poe might have stopped there, just as he might have ended "The
Raven" with the sixteenth stanza. The narrative is complete, and
there are even "morals" or "lessons" for those who demand them.
But, as Poe says in "The Philosophy of Composition,"

> in subjects so handled, however skilfully, or with however vivid an
> array of incident, there is always a certain hardness or nakedness,
> which repels the artistical eye. Two things are invariably required—
> first, some amount of complexity, or more properly, adaptation; and,
> secondly, some amount of suggestiveness—some undercurrent, how-
> ever indefinite, of meaning.

[24] Charles O'Donnell, in "From Earth to Ether: Poe's Flight into Space,"
PMLA, LXXVII (March 1962), pp. 88, 89, makes much the same point in
his discussion of *The Narrative of Arthur Gordon Pym*. O'Donnell speaks of
blood as "the life force" and as "suggestive of life, mystery, suffering, terror
—in general of the human situation."

[25] "The angel which I saw stand upon the sea and upon the earth . . . sware
. . . that there should be time no longer" (Revelation 10:5,6).

To achieve complexity and suggestiveness, Poe added two stanzas to "The Raven." To "The Masque of the Red Death" he added two sentences: "And the flames of the tripods expired. And Darkness and Decay and the Red Death held illimitable dominion over all."

"Let there be light" was one of the principles of Creation; darkness, then, is a principle of Chaos. And to Poe Chaos is synonymous with Nothingness, "which, to all finite perception, Unity must be." Decay occurs as matter "expels the ether" to return to or to sink into Unity. Prince Prospero's world, created out of a chaos ruled by the Red Death, returns to chaos, ruled by the trinity of Darkness and Decay and the Red Death. But, it will be remembered, Prince Prospero's world came into being *because of* the Red Death, which, although it includes death, is the principle of life. In Chaos, then, is the promise of new lives and of new worlds which will swell into existence and then, in their turn, subside into nothingness in the eternal process of contraction and expansion which Poe describes in *Eureka*.[26]

There are "morals" implicit and explicit in this interpretation of "The Masque of the Red Death," but they need not be underlined here. Poe, who had maintained in his "Review of Nathaniel Hawthorne's *Twice-Told Tales*" that "Truth is often, and in very great degree, the aim of the tale," was working with a larger, but surely not entirely inexpressible, truth than can be conveyed in a simple "Poor Richard" maxim; and in that task, it seems to me, he transcends the tale (into which classification most critics put "The Masque of the Red Death") to create a prose which, in its free rhythms, its diction, its compression, and its suggestion, approaches poetry.[27]

[26] Poe's theories of the universe, including his theory of the identity of Unity and Nothingness, are explained in detail in *Eureka*. Also pertinent is Poe's statement in *Eureka* that "In the Original Unity of the First Thing lies the Secondary Cause of All Things, with the Germ of their Inevitable Annihilation."

[27] Poe calls *Eureka* a prose poem, "Shadow" a parable, and "Silence" a fable. Both "Shadow" and "Silence" have many of the qualities of prose poetry. According to Buranelli (p. 113), Poe believed that "prose poetry is genuine poetry; intellectually inpoverished rhyme is not." Blair (p. 238) also notes that the indefiniteness and suggestiveness of "The Masque of the Red Death" are "calculated to elevate the soul"—and elevation of the soul is, according to Poe, the function of poetry.

The ideas that were haunting Poe when he published *Eureka* were already haunting him in 1842, when he published "The Masque of the Red Death," and what emerged was not, certainly, a short story; nor was it, except by the freest definition, a tale. For either category, it is deficient in plot and in characterization. Instead, "The Masque of the Red Death" combines elements of the parable and of the myth. Not as explicit or as pointedly allegorical always as the parable, "The Masque of the Red Death" nevertheless can be (and has been) read as a parable of the inevitability and the universality of death; but it deals also with the feats of a hero or demigod—Prospero—and with Poe's concepts of universal principles, and it has the mystery and the remoteness of myth. What Poe has created, then, is a kind of mythic parable, brief and poetic, of the human condition, of man's fate, and of the fate of the universe.

An Introduction to *Pym*

by Sidney Kaplan

They who dream by day are cognizant of many things which escape those who dream only by night. In their grey visions they obtain glimpses of eternity, and thrill, in awaking, to find that they have been upon the verge of the great secret. In snatches, they learn something of the wisdom which is of good, and more of the mere knowledge which is of evil. They penetrate, however rudderless or compassless, into the vast ocean of the "light ineffable" and again, like the adventurers of the Nubian geographer, *"agressi sunt mare tenebrarum, quid in eo esset exploraturi."* (Poe's "Eleanora," 1842).

The Narrative of Arthur Gordon Pym of Nantucket, published in New York during the summer of 1838, is in some ways Poe's plainest and most enigmatic story. It is the only long piece of fiction he ever wrote. As poet, critic, and teller of tales grotesque and arabesque, he had already made his mark as a "magazinist," when, in March 1836, James Kirke Paulding, who had just completed a weighty defense of American slavery, suggested that it might be worth his while to "undertake a Tale in a couple of volumes." In June Harper's turned down his *Tales of the Folio Club,* advising that American readers preferred "a single and connected story" of book length. Poe went quickly to work. Six months later the first three chapters of *Pym* appeared in the *Southern Literary Messenger.*

While in England *Pym* had a small success as hoax (the London editor deleted its terminal white god), in the United States, although Horace Greeley was taken in, the book fell flat as a narra-

"An Introduction to *Pym*" (original title: "Introduction") by Sidney Kaplan. From the American Century Series edition of *The Narrative of Arthur Gordon Pym* by Edgar Allan Poe © 1960 by Hill and Wang, Inc. Reprinted by permission of Hill & Wang and the author.

tive of real or imagined adventure.[1] To its final allegorical riddle, as far as the record shows, everyone was either blind or indifferent. Almost totally ignored by the reviewers, *Pym* was slashed in Philadelphia by Burton's *Gentleman's Magazine:* whereas "the voyages of Gulliver were politically satirical," Gordon Pym's travels were an "impudent attempt at humbugging the public." A few years later Poe himself, in a letter to Burton, referred to *Pym* as "a very silly book." When in 1849, the year Poe died, Rufus Griswold, his literary executor—in a double sense—grumbled that the concocter of *Pym* had tried to give it *Robinson Crusoe*'s "air of truth," but had succeeded only in compiling "as liberal an array of paining and revolting horrors as ever was invented by Ann Radcliffe," he was probably echoing the popular view. As one Nathaniel Ames, who, a few years before *Pym,* had authored his own *Nautical Reminiscences,* put it, every barber's clerk who crossed the ocean favored the public with his memoirs.

A century has passed and *Pym*'s stock is steadily rising on the critical exchange; it may almost be said that a minor *"Pym* boom," stemming in part from Baudelaire's early worship of Poe, is now under way on both sides of the water.

For Baudelaire, Poe had many virtues, but "more important than anything else" was that in "a century infatuated with itself," this "child of a nation more infatuated with itself than all others" had "imperturbably affirmed the natural wickedness . . . the primordial perversity of man." Against all the "misguided equalitarians," Poe had proclaimed that "we are all born marked for evil." A year after *Les Fleurs du Mal,* Baudelaire embarked on a labor of love—a translation of *Pym*—about which he wrote to Sainte-Beuve: "You, who so love profundities, why not investigate the profundities of Edgar Poe?" A "purely realistic," "purely human book," in which the "genius of the author" reveled in "terrible scenes and in amazing descriptions of islands and tribes not shown on any map"—so Baudelaire assessed the "admirable novel" on which he planned to write some "Last Notes on Edgar Poe" to preface his translation of *Pym.*

[1] Alfred Russel Wallace, the evolutionist, wrote to a friend: ". . . the Antarctic part completely spoils it, being so completely impossible, with its abundant vegetation, mild climate, fruits and land animals near the *South Pole!* Also the fantastic idea of *striped water* so utterly unnecessary . . . it was these absurdities that disgusted me with the story."

Twenty years later, in his *French Poets and Novelists,* the early Henry James, who had no use for Baudelaire's "lurid landscape and unclean furniture," took occasion to demur. For Americans, James thought, Baudelaire was "compromised by his having made himself the apostle of our own Edgar Poe." Although Poe, "much the greater charlatan of the two," was the "greater genius," to take him with "more than a certain degree of seriousness" was to "lack seriousness one's self." Indeed, an enthusiasm for Poe was the "mark of a decidedly primitive stage of reflection. . . ." As for *Pym,* although the problematical Prince Amerigo of *The Golden Bowl* could remember the tale as showing "what imagination Americans *could* have," a few years later, speaking in his own voice in the preface to *The Altar of the Dead,* James would finally see *Pym* as without "intrinsic values," its "imaginative effort wasted."

Years before, in Baltimore, at the public reburial of Poe's bones, another American writer, feeling "a strong impulse" to be present "in memory of Poe," had hobbled to the platform, but refused a eulogy. In social talk after the ceremony was over, old Walt Whitman reminisced about Poe.

> For a long while, and until lately, I had a distaste for Poe's writings. I wanted, and still want for poetry, the clear sun shining, and fresh air blowing—the strength and power of health, not of delirium, even amid the stormiest passions—with always the background of the eternal moralities. Non-complying with these requirements, Poe's genius has yet conquer'd a special recognition for itself, and I too have come to fully admit it, and appreciate it and him.

In a dream he had once had, Whitman went on, he saw a vessel at midnight in a storm.

> It was no great full-rigg'd ship, nor majestic steamer, steering firmly through the gale, but seem'd one of those superb little schooner yachts . . . flying uncontroll'd with torn sails and broken spars through the wild sleet and winds and waves of the night. On the deck was a slender, slight, beautiful figure, a dim man, apparently enjoying all the terror, the murk and the dislocation of which he was the center and the victim. That figure of my lurid dream might stand for Edgar Poe, his spirit, his fortunes, and his poems—themselves all lurid dreams.

Was Whitman evoking the figure of Gordon Pym at the helm of the dismasted *Ariel* (Shelley's boat), flying through the stormy Atlantic night? There is sorrow and tenderness in this image of Poe, but five years later, as he approached the grave, in a New Year's memorandum on "Edgar Poe's Significance" (beginning with the un-Whitmanian words: "In diagnosing this disease called human- ity"), while crediting Poe with an "intense faculty for technical and abstract beauty," Whitman spoke his last word on the subject: "Al- most without the first sign of moral principle, or of the concrete or its heroisms, or the simpler affections of the heart," Poe had "an in- corrigible propensity toward nocturnal themes, a demoniac under- tone behind every page—and, by final judgment probably belongs among the electric lights of imaginative literature, brilliant and dazzling, but with no heat."

Pym's critics of the past quarter century have followed Baudelaire —and Freud—rather than James or Whitman. For Marie Bona- parte, psychoanalyzing Poe under the cautious imprimatur of the master, "all the depth of the tale . . . resembles the latent content of the dream" [2]—a lead picked up by W. H. Auden, who, apprais- ing *Pym* as one of the finest stories of "pure adventure" ever written, "an object lesson in the art," describes its protagonist as a "hero" who is "as purely passive as the I in dreams." More recently, Patrick J. Quinn has also found *Pym* to be a "profoundly oneiric drama," a masterly integration of "the theme of deception with the pattern of revolt"—a criminally neglected classic from which Melville cribbed, without acknowledgment, in writing *Moby Dick*. It is "the intense death-wish," declares Quinn, which is the defining character- istic in the personality of Pym: "With his great imagination of dis- aster, Poe integrates the evil of men and the evil inherent in the nature of the material universe. . . ." Nor does another full-dress study of Poe lower this high value placed on *Pym*. A "minor but hitherto unacknowledged masterpiece"; a "symbolic enactment of man's search for logic and meaning"; an excursion into "a philoso- phy of knowledge"—thus does Edward H. Davidson laud the tale of a "curiously 'American hero,' uprooted, and yet determined to

---

[2] In his introduction to her *Edgar Poe: Étude Psychanalytique* (1933) Freud wrote: "Investigations such as this do not claim to explain creative genius, but they do reveal the factors which awaken it and the sort of subject matter it is destined to choose."

know himself." In a "mindless, chaotic world the only final reality
is the single perceiving self."

> The search for the self is the loss of the self; the quest is the annihila-
> tion. To remain in ignorance is to maintain one's primal being; to
> be curious is to be suicidal. The world of reality constantly under-
> goes this cyclic metamorphosis, from life to death and back to life
> again; but man, though a creature submissive to the natural laws
> around him, can go only through death or perhaps to . . . the silence
> of total annihilation.

Finally, in Harry Levin's recent study of *The Power of Blackness*
—which has so far spoken the most revealing words about the tale—
Pym's voyage is a part of "The American Nightmare," a "Journey
to the End of the Night."

Whether these critics have spoken rightly or wrongly of *Pym* as
a whole, each reader will, of course, decide for himself. For three
quarters of its pages, Poe's tale is perhaps plain—and brilliant—
enough, and this preface will not offer a disquisition on the sources
that Poe ransacked to give verisimilitude to Pym's travels. Let the
warning suffice, as Bryant once said, to be on guard against "profound researches into things already sufficiently clear": the realism
of Pym's trials in queer settings may be a gambit to establish a "will-
ing suspension of disbelief" in the allegory to which they lead. Nor
may it be bad policy to hearken to Poe's answer given to an editor
who, shortly before *Pym* appeared, questioned the nature of his
effects in the ghoulish horrors of "Berenice": "You ask me in what
this nature consists? In the ludicrous heightened into the grotesque;
the fearful colored into the horrible; the witty exaggerated into the
burlesque; the singular wrought out into the strange and mystical."

*   *   *

It is the concluding portion of *Pym*—the "Incredible Adventures
and Discoveries Still Farther South," as Poe put it on his title page
—which, it might be argued, was conceived by itself and tacked on
at the end, that to the ordinary reader more than a century later may
not be sufficiently clear. "There have been critics who object to
what they are pleased to call an inconclusive ending," wrote Arthur
Hobson Quinn in his "critical" biography of Poe twenty years ago.

"But when the details of the voyages have long been forgotten, the picture of the mysterious figure remains, stimulating the imagination of those readers who do not have to have everything explained to them in words of one syllable." Regrettably, there have been other readers, less knowing, who have been puzzled by the great white image—and the black ones that precede it—at the close of *Pym*. Better perhaps to proceed, as did Sir Thomas Browne, who was fascinated by Pliny's account of the waters of Siberis, which blackened the skin and frizzed the hair of white men—who held, "What songs the Syrens sang, or what name Achilles assumed when he hid himself among women, though puzzling questions, are not beyond *all* conjecture." The solver of the end of *Barnaby Rudge* liked nothing more than a cryptogram, either one to be fashioned or decoded, and it was Poe himself, even as he began work on *Pym,* who held that "unity of effect" was not "indispensable" in "the common novel," which is "admired for its detached passages, without reference to the work as a whole—or . . . any general design. . . ."

What then is the meaning of the "secret writing" that Edgar Allan Poe fashioned and Arthur Gordon Pym of Edgartown found in the black fauna and flora of his mysterious Antarctic, in the black teeth of his black devils, in the polar water like warm milk, in the portentous words carved on the skeleton of the earth?

During the fall of 1833 the *Baltimore Sunday Visiter* awarded a hundred dollars to Poe for his prize story, "MS. Found in a Bottle." At the close of this brief tale, a familiar Poeian hero, haunted by "nervous restlessness," finds himself aboard a ghost ship, which, drawn by an "impetuous undertow," is hurtling south through "colossal waters" in the "blackness of eternal night." Although he is filled with horror, "yet a curiosity to penetrate the mysteries of these awful regions" triumphs over his despair. In his MS he notes: "It is evident that we are hurrying onward to some exciting knowledge—some never-to-be-imparted secret, whose attainment is destruction. Perhaps this current leads us to the southern pole itself." Unlike Pym, this hero does not live to impart his secret: the white ice "opens suddenly" and the ship descends madly into the maelstrom of the "supernatural sea." A note that Poe appended to the tale a few years later relates that he has since become "acquainted with the maps of Mercator, in which the ocean is represented as rushing, by four mouths into the (northern) Polar Gulf, to be absorbed into the bowels of the earth; the Pole itself being represented by a black rock, towering to a prodigious height." What was this "exciting knowledge," this "never-to-be-imparted secret"? Was Poe simply indulging his penchant for mystification?

The note on Mercator is suggestive of another spur to the imagination that created *Pym*. When Poe was a boy of nine, an ex-captain of infantry, one John Cleves Symmes, living in St. Louis, addressed to "all the World" a printed circular which he sent to learned societies and distinguished persons in America and Europe. "I declare the earth is hollow and habitable within . . . that it is open at the poles"—so began the manifesto that called for "one hundred brave companions," to hop off from Siberia for the North Pole, where, Symmes guaranteed, they would find "a warm and rich land stocked with thrifty vegetables and animals, if not men. . . ." The theory of "Symmes' Hole"—so Thoreau refers to it in *Walden*—was bandied about in the United States for a quarter of a century; the captain's son, Americus Symmes, tells us that it was "overwhelmed with ridicule as the production of a distempered imagination, or the result of partial insanity"—a "fruitful source of jest with the newspapers."

But the captain did have his champions. One of these, a pseudonymous shipmaster, Adam Seaborn, two years after Symmes had called on Sir Humphry Davy and Baron Alexander von Humboldt as "protectors," responded in a roughhewn Gulliverian novel whose title was *Symzonia: A Voyage of Discovery*. In two basic ways Seaborn edited Symmes: first, his voyage was to the Antarctic; second, at the South Pole, or rather within it, he found men. Indeed, Symzonia, as he called the place, was "the abode of a race perfect in their kind." What amazes Seaborn more than anything else about the appearance of his polar Utopians is that they are perfectly white: "the sootiest African does not differ more from us in darkness of skin and grossness of features than they did from me in fairness of complexion and delicacy of form." On the conscious level Seaborn was suggesting no racist theory of color; in one of his final comments on the excellence of the Symzonians he makes the point that they are as fond of nature's freely given fruits as Americans are of those which are "wrung from the bloody sweat of slavery." Yet is it surprising that for an American, citizen of a land in which slaves are black, heir of a Christian moral-chromatic tradition in which God is white and the devil black, that the Perfect should be White?

Did Poe know the theory of Symmes? Without a doubt. Was he familiar with Seaborn's book? Probably. The work of another who believed in "holes at the Poles" he knew well. In April 1836, Jeremiah N. Reynolds, who a year after *Pym* would tell a story about Mocha Dick (like the Ethiopian Albino, as white as wool), urged Congress, in the House of Representatives, to explore the South Seas. In the issue of the *Messenger* that carried the first installment of *Pym,* Poe praised Reynolds' speech; indeed, he had already borrowed material from it for the tale. Reynolds was a public defender of Symmes. Years later, as Poe gasped his last breath in Baltimore, in his delirium he called loudly for "Reynolds."

The black rock that marked the North Pole ("Rupes nigra et altissima," Mercator labels it on his map of 1569); the hollow earth of Captain Symmes; the Antarctic Utopia of the Perfect Whites; from these in part Poe constructed—what shall we call it?—his Pymzonia, his world of Black and White, whose "exciting knowledge," undisclosed in "MS Found in a Bottle," will lurk in *Pym*'s chiaroscuro arabesque. "While . . . I cannot but lament the most unfortunate and bloody events which immediately arose from my advice," the Nantucket lad reflects after persuading the captain of the *Jane Guy* to solve "the great problem" of the Antarctic, "I must still be allowed to feel some degree of gratification at having been instrumental, however remotely, in opening to the eye of science one of the most intensely exciting secrets which has ever engrossed its attention."

Critics during the past half century, answering Poe's challenge, have now and then tried to discover the exciting secret of Tsalal and the Great White Avenger. For Henry James, thinking of *Pym* as a ghost story like "The Turn of the Screw," there was, in a sense, no secret at all. The "would-be portentous climax . . . where the indispensable history is absent, where the phenomena evoked, the moving accidents, coming straight . . . are immediate and flat, and the attempt is all at the horrific in itself" is a failure because it stops short. Concluded James: "There *are* no connections; not only . . . in the sense of further statement, but of our own further relation to the elements, which hang in the void: whereby we see the effect lost, the imaginative effort wasted"—a judgment to which F. O. Matthiessen objected, pointing out that in "the mirror that James has held up to Poe's narrative he has not caught the horror of its unrelieved light, which had been the main intention of Poe's climax." For S. Foster Damon, "the nature of the horrible whiteness which sucked Gordon Pym down to his death [!] at the South Pole" was "the same whiteness which, incarnate as Moby Dick, rose from the depths and all but killed Ishmael." Poe recorded "a mental voyage which had brought him to the edge of the unknown and to a point where he must find a new set of terms for what he tremblingly descried beyond that edge," thought Edward Shanks. In *Pym*'s last pages "realism turns to frank fantasy"; when Poe finished, "he was conscious that, after many and cruel misfortunes, he was hurrying into an awful obscurity, able only to guess at its nature, helpless to save himself from it." Less vague was Marie Bonaparte, in whose ears the names of Tsalal sounded "like infant babble," the direction of whose analysis may perhaps be seen in a montage of passages:

> . . . the black island represents a *cloacal* phantasy . . . *white* has reactivated memory traces of infantile masturbation in Nu-Nu's unconscious . . . pleasurable but vague feelings akin to those produced by tickling (*"Tekeli-li"*) . . . a terror of white, of milk color, among the natives of Tsalal, whose incest wishes and sexuality appear to have been . . . precociously suppressed . . . the strangers' apparently milk-stained teeth implying incestuous relations with the mother.

To whose vengeance did Poe finally refer? asked Bonaparte. The vengeance of the father was her answer:

> For he in fact it was, who, in prehistoric times established his taboos on the isle of *Tsalal*. His prohibitions . . . hold the black wicked sons from approaching the *whiteness* of the mother. . . . Thus the epilogue to this story ends with a concrete though sibylline reference to the father, from whom every primitive taboo, and our own morals derive.

Whereas James could make out "no connections" in Pym's end, critics of the past decade find the meaning and virtue of the allegory precisely in its "No Exit" quality. Patrick Quinn sees *Pym*'s chief merit in its taking us "from the most pedestrian of beginnings to the most weirdly impressive of endings"; we are simply confronted at the end with the enigma of Pym's final vision. . . . Throughout the last vertiginous chapters of his story Poe multiplies the details which culminate in this cryptic apparition. . . . But at no point does Poe stop to read these signs. They retain the clouded complexity of dream images, composite of dread and longing.

Dread of whom? Longing for what? Another critic, Edward Davidson, tries to be more specific. The end of the book, he maintains, is

either absurd, monstrous, or mysterious; for all that happens is a voyage in an oversize canoe into a blinding white light near the South Pole—as if Poe had no more to say and thus stopped his narrative short; he even increased the insult by adding an appendix in small type in which he essayed to clarify certain confusions—and clarified nothing.

At the end of his journey, concludes Davidson, Pym is sailing toward

that whiteness whose center lies beyond first things and whose nexus may be the creative impulse of the universe itself. Faced with this bewildering and ultimate reduction, Poe can use only one word, an idea of whiteness, the negation of fact and shape. Melville's Ishmael came back from this side of the ultimate illumination; but Pym went all the way through and never returned. He, like the primal order of matter itself, was reduced to a blinding One—or chaos. There was no word or term which could further report the vision of nothing on the other side. Nothing was all; there was no other word for it but "white."

Would Poe, the supremely conscious artist of our literature, have agreed with any or all of these interpretations? Perhaps a reading of the allegory, less Freudian, less existentialist, less oneiric, will turn up a surer meaning at the level of Poe's intention.

Poe—whom Valéry called "that great literary engineer"—once described his literary method as follows: ". . . having conceived with deliberate care, a certain unique or single effect to be wrought out, [the writer] then invents such incidents—he then combines such events as may best aid him in establishing this preconceived effect." At another time, arguing against Coleridge, he would write: "The fancy as nearly creates as the imagination, and neither at all. Novel conceptions are merely unusual combinations. The mind of man can imagine nothing which does not really exist; if it could, it would create not only ideally but substantially as do the thoughts of God."

The world of Tsalal is black to its core—so quintessentially black that it is divided by "chasmal differences" from whiteness in any form. The sea around it is "extraordinarily dark"; its fauna and flora are black; its granite and soil, the very dust in the bowels of its earth are black. Although Pym discovers white arrow flints in the chasms, he stresses the fact that there are "no light-colored substances of any kind upon the island." All this is passing strange. Not so strange, however, are the natives of the black world: "They were about the ordinary stature of Europeans, but of a more muscular and brawny frame. Their complexion a jet black, with thick and long wooly hair." The black women have "personal beauty" and a grace "not to be found in civilized society." The lips of the blacks are "thick and clumsy"; they have black teeth. Years after *Pym,* Poe wrote to a friend:

> Monk Lewis once was asked how he came . . . to introduce *black* banditti, when, in the country where the scene was laid, black people were quite unknown. His answer was: "I introduced them because I truly anticipated that blacks would have more *effect* on my audience than whites—and if I had taken it into my head that, by making them sky-blue the effect would have been greater, why sky-blue they should have been."

But it is not to create an effect of the totally fantastic that the banditti of Tsalal are black. In all, they are not different, except for their teeth—from the pure Negroes of Georgia or Virginia. Pym notes that when they are amused they clap their hands, slap their thighs and breasts, and laugh uproariously—and their favorite food is tame fowl. The image is the American stereotype of the minstrel Negro. Indeed, as Levin points out, the first view of the island is of a ledge that reminds Pym of another South, for it bears a "strong resemblance to corded bales of cotton." [3]

The name of the black island is Tsalal, the Hebrew verb for "to be dark"; its principal town is Klock-Klock, the Hebrew for "to be black"; its chief is Too-Wit, the Hebrew for "to be dirty"; the king of the archipelago is Tsalemon, the Hebrew for "shady." Poe knew little Hebrew; while writing *Pym,* when he needed a few Hebrew words for a review of a volume of Arabian travels he applied for help to a learned professor of New York. Why then invent names in

---

[3] I have ignored the "problem" of the half-breed Peters—as Poe does in a way. At one point Pym remarks: "We were the only living white men on the island."

the Biblical tongue? Was it simply play—another experiment in cryptography, of which he was so fond? "As we can scarcely imagine a time when there did not exist a necessity, or at least a desire, of transmitting information from one individual to another in such a manner as to elude general comprehension," he would later note, "so we may well suppose the practice of writing in cipher to be of great antiquity." Perhaps there is a hint of such mystification in these names; even to those who knew no Hebrew, Tsalemon sounded vaguely like Solomon. And there was a special effect in the whole idea: here were blacks, very like the slaves one saw in Virginia, speaking the language of Genesis. Was there also a deeper theory of language at work in Poe's choice, one that abused Emerson to make a point? "Albert, in his Hebrew Dictionary," he remarks in one of the "Pinakidia" printed in the *Messenger* as he is grinding out *Pym*, "pretends to discover in each word, in its root, in its letters, and in the manner of pronouncing them, the reason of its signification. Leescher in his treatise *De causis Linguae Hebreae,* carries the matter even farther." So, in Tsalal, the word is the thing—both were created together; and the word is in the language of the creation itself. *"Nullus enim locus sine genio est,"* he would cite from Servius as epigraph for "The Island of the Fay," continuing: "I love, indeed, to regard the dark valleys, and the grey rocks, and the waters that silently smile . . . I love to regard these as themselves but the colossal members of one vast animate and sentient whole— a whole whose . . . thought is that of God. . . ." How avid he was to pursue this line of thought may be seen in another of the "Pinakidia," where, pondering the black water of Tsalal, he writes: "The stream flowing through the middle of the Valley of Jehoshaphat is called, in the Gospel of St. John, 'the brook of cedars.' In the Septuagint the word is κέδρον, darkness, from the Hebrew Kiddar, black. . . ."

And not only are the names of the Tsalalians Hebrew; they speak a kind of Hebrew too. When the white handkerchief on Captain Guy's oar stops the black paddlers, they exclaim "Anamoo-moo! Lama-Lama!"—"What ship is this? What evil sent by God upon the water?" At sight of anything white the blacks, in fear, scream "Tekeli-li!"—as do the white birds who scare Nu-Nu ("to deny") to death. "Mene, Mene, Tekel, Upharsin"—so read the handwriting on the wall, the words that Daniel deciphered. "Tekel"—"Thou art weighed in the balances, and art found wanting"—so Daniel revealed God's word to Belshazzar, who was slain that night. When Captain Guy asks malevolent Too-Wit why his men do not carry arms, he replies, "mattee non we pa pa si"—"There is no need of arms when all are brothers"—the last five words of which are an obvious macaronic of Latin, English, and Italian, while the first is the Hebrew for "spear." To be sure, the "great men" among the Tsalalians are Wampoos or Yampoos—a blend of Swift's Yahoos and the race of Ham, one of whose sons was Cush, in the Septuagint called Ethiops—that same Ham whose posterity (as Genesis has it) occupied the southernmost regions of the world.

The black Tsalalians are very wicked folk. It is not merely that Too-Wit is the cunning savage who howls and kills in the potboilers of Pacific adventure common in Poe's day. Like Seymour, the brutal black cook of the "realistic" part of the tale, he is "in all respects" no less than a "perfect demon." The Tsalalians, says Pym, are "the most barbarous, subtle, and bloodthirsty wretches that ever contaminated" the earth; and again, more forcefully, "the most wicked, hypocritical, vindictive, bloodthirsty, and altogether fiendish race of men upon the face of the globe." The Tsalalians, in fact, are the people of the Prince of Darkness. They do not fear the "formidable" serpents that cross their path; they pronounce the names of their land and king with a "prolonged hissing sound." Tsalal is Hell; its water is Styx, a kind of dirty, imperfect blood flowing thickly "in distinct veins, each of a distinct hue," which do not commingle. The color of the water is "every possible shade of purple"—"*persa,*" as Dante, whom Poe knew in the Italian, describes it in the *Inferno.*[4] "The phenomena of this water," notes Pym, "formed the first definite link in that vast chain of apparent miracles with which I was destined to be at length encircled."

Tsalal is in the Antarctic, yet its landscape (despite a touch of the cotton South) is a blend of the terrains of Ethiopia, Sinai, and ruined Babylon. Its patterned gorges, reminiscent of the church of Abba Libanos hewn from the Ethiopian rock, traces out an Ethiopian word. On the black granite walls are carved Arabic and Egyp-

[4] Why purple? In 1845, as the first of his "Fifty Suggestions" printed in *Graham's Magazine,* Poe wrote: "Your 'blue' . . . is black in *issimo—'nigrum nigrius nigro'*—like the matter from which Raymond Lully first manufactured his alcohol."

tian letters, reminiscent of the writing on the Sinaitic rocks that
so tantalized travelers passing through Arabia Petraea—whose ac-
counts Poe read and reviewed as he wrote *Pym*. In the literature of
Ethiopian travel—articles in encyclopedias like the *Britannica* and
Rees's popular work, books by David Bruce and Job Ludolphus,
Pliny's *Natural History* (which he used as a source for "Siope—A
Fable," a sketch of 1837)—he had read of the mountains that "assume
wild and fantastic forms, with sides frequently abrupt and precip-
itous . . . only accessible by very difficult passes," and of the Blue
River, with its rocky formations "from the first to the last degree
of the geological table"; of the Niger, so called by the Hebrews and
Greeks "because it runs with black and muddy water," preserving its
blackness even as it flows through Lake Tzanicum, coursing "through
wildernesses full of black dust . . . cliffs and craggy rocks . . .
scorched and burnt," where Ethiopians lived—some of whom
"looked upon the sun . . . as their implacable enemy." And it was
in Ethiopia that the rulers were descended from Solomon (Tsalemon) and Sheba—the same Sheba who gave to Solomon a gift of
that black wood from which Poe wrought the clubs of the Tsalalians.
When, driven by hunger, Pym stumbles on a place of singular wild-
ness, "strewn with huge tumuli apparently the wreck of some gigantic structures of art," there come into his mind "the descriptions
given by travellers of those dreary regions marking the site of degraded Babylon"—founded by the line of Ham.

The Enemy of the Tsalalians is Whiteness—whether it be the
"Four Beasts in One" furred in the white ermine of judgeship (a
visitor, like the red-eyed polar bear from the World of Whiteness),
an egg, an open book, a pan of flour—or white men, from whose
complexion the blacks "recoil." [5] "Tekeli-li!" the blacks cry out in
"mingled horror, rage, and intense curiosity" when the chromatic
icon of their damnation appears before them. It is the eternal hostility of black and white, figured forth when, in the beginning, "God
divided the light from the darkness" and "formed man of the dust
of the ground"—in the case of the Tsalalians, whose name is their

[5] In a note hidden away in a scholarly journal, Mrs. Mozelle S. Allen points
out that Poe, a reader of Voltaire, describes the white snow of divinity that falls
on Pym as a "fine white powder, resembling ashes," and that in Voltaire's *History of the Voyages of Scarmantado* the black pirate lectures to his white cap-
tive: "You have a long nose and we have a flat nose; your hair is wholly straight
and our wool is curly; you have skin the color of ashes [*cendre*] and ours is the
color of ebony; consequently, we ought, by the sacred laws of nature, to be
enemies."

meaning, from the black dust, three or four inches deep, on the floor of the chasms. "Enter into the rock, and hide thee in the dust," warned Isaiah, "for fear of the Lord and for the glory of His majesty." Poe will write it all, on the day of creation, into the very foundations of the universe.

As Pym explores the "perfect regularity" of the winding chasms at the bottom of the black pit he can scarcely bring himself to believe that the formations are "the work of nature." How then were the chasms made? Apparently by a careful, miraculous cleavage of the bedrock, for there are "minor cavities in the sides . . . each cavity having a corresponding protuberance opposite." It is the "Tekel" written by God's hand in and on the walls of the chasms, in the letters of the ancients, that decrees the timeless antipathy. Contrary to some critical opinion, the word that Poe says is the Ethiopian verbal root "to be shady" is not a hoax but a real Ethiopian word, the equivalent, in fact, as Poe ascertained in the *Lexicon* of Gesenius (published in Boston as he wrote *Pym*) of the Hebrew "Tsalal." [6] And the same is true of the Arabic "to be white" (Gesenius gives it as "to be dazzling white") and of the Egyptian (Coptic) "The Region of the South"—all chipped, wonderfully, in single pieces by a supernatural hand from the black stone.

But what of the "human form," whose arm outstretched toward

[6] Edward Robinson, *A Hebrew and English Lexicon of the Old Testament from the Latin of William Gesenius* (1836). This lexicon was Poe's source for all or most of the Hebrew, Arabic, Ethiopian, and Coptic words he manipulated in *Pym*. Two of the trickiest occur in the mysterious "Note" that closes the book:

Figure 1, then Figure 2, Figure 3, and Figure 5, when conjoined with one another in the precise order which the chasms themselves presented, and when deprived of the small lateral branches or arches . . . constitute an Ethiopian verbal root—the root ደለመ 'To be shady'—whence all the inflections of shadow or darkness. . . . The upper range is evidently the Arabic verbal root ܩܠܐ 'To be white,' whence all the inflections of brilliancy and whiteness. The following reproductions of the corresponding definitions in the lexicon (pp. 865, 868-69) reveal how Poe worked his source.

צָלַל Arab. ظَلَّ , *to be shaded, dark,* Neh. 13: 19.

צֶלֶם obsol. root, Aeth. ደለመ: *to be shady,* Arab. ظَلِمَ to be obscure, dark, ظُلْمَة darkness.

צָחַר obsol. root, Arab. ܨܚܘ Conj. XI, to be dazzling white. Kindr. is

צָחֹר see under צָחַר . — Hence

צַחַר m. *whiteness* sc. of wool Ez. 27: 18.

the south, ordains the sacred division: "to be shady"—"to be white"?
Among the "Pinakidia" in the *Messenger* of August 1836, Poe notes
that in "the Dutch Vondel's tragedy, 'The Deliverance of the Children of Israel,' one of the principal characters is the Divinity himself." In the closing line of *Pym* this Divinity speaks: *"I have graven
it within the hills, and my vengeance upon the dust within the
rock."* *These* words *are* a hoax, but only in a certain sense are they
meant to deceive.[7] The passage, quoted, sounds as if it comes from
Scripture; in fact, it was written by Poe, who, in another tale, would
engrave on an African stone the words "DESOLATION" and
"SILENCE." The "I" in the passage is the "human figure" of the
chasm. Both are Jehovah, who also not rarely wrote his word on
stone. "Ethiopia shall soon stretch out her hands unto God"—so
the Abolitionists untiringly quoted from the sixty-eighth Psalm; but
the outstretched hand of the god of the chasm reaches out to the
region of whiteness. "And now we rushed into the embraces of the
cataract, where a chasm threw itself open to receive us. But there
arose in our pathway a shrouded human figure, very far larger in its
proportions than any dweller among men. And the hue of the skin
of the figure was of the perfect whiteness of the snow." Pym feels no
terror; unlike the hero of "MS Found in a Bottle," who descends in
horror into the whirlpool, Gordon Pym, lulled in warm milk (it
was Jonathan Edwards who said that milk, by its "whiteness and
purity," was the image of "the word of God from the breasts of the
church"), rushes away from the Black into the embracing arms of
the comforting White, while the gigantic white birds shriek God's
"Tekel" and Nu-Nu dies of fright. Why should Pym feel terror at
the sight of Daniel's Ancient of Days, whose garment was as white
as snow, and the hair of his head like pure wool"? Or of the white
Divinity whose voice, in the Vision of St. John, is as "the sound of
many waters" and whose raiment, as St. Matthew saw it, was "white
as the light"? For Melville, in his discourse on "The Whiteness of
the Whale," behind the whiteness of the Divine, there lurked "an
elusive something in the innermost idea of this hue, which strikes

[7] Many years ago, George Edward Woodberry pointed out another manipula-
tion by Poe of a similar kind: "A more curious instance of Poe's dealing with
authorities is his note on *Israfel*, which originally read, 'And the angel Israfel,
who has the sweetest voice of all God's creatures: *Koran*.' The passage referred
to is not in the Koran, but in Sale's *Preliminary Discourses* (iv, 71). Poe derived
it from the notes to Moore's Lalla Rookh. . . ." Bayard Taylor in his *Diver-
sions of the Echo Club* describes an "intellectual diversion" of Poe's time:
"spurious quotations from various languages."

more of panic to the soul than that redness which affrights in
blood." In *Pym,* it is blackness that affrights; for Poe the Revelation
(II:17) was of a different order: "To him that overcometh will I
give to eat of the hidden manna, and will give him a white stone,
and in the stone a new name written, which no man knoweth saving
he that receiveth it." Is it worthy of note that it is on the opening
day of spring that Pym is taken by the white god?

Revelation is precisely what Poe is after. To those who have
viewed him as an archetypal Rimbaud or Sartre it may come as a
surprise that Poe was a Biblical fundamentalist of the most orthodox
sort. Reviewing John L. Stephens' *Arabia Petraea* while *Pym* was in
the works, what he singled out of principal value was its "direct
tendency to throw light upon the Book of Books": by "dissipating
the obscurities and determining the exact sense of the Scriptures"
it could serve as an "instrument in the downfall of unbelief." In a
piece of hack work on "Palaestine," written a few months before, he
had already viewed the blasted deserts of the Holy Land as "the visible effects of divine displeasure." Now, speaking with approval of
Alexander Keith's *Evidence of Prophecy,* which defended the "long
continued slavery of the Africans" as the curse on Ham, Poe saw
in Stephens' book an argument for "the *literalness* of the understanding of the Bible predictions as an *essential* feature of prophecy." But there was in the Bible no prophecy of black damnation
clear enough for his needs, and he therefore wrote his own: *"I have
graven it within the hills. . . ."*

Does all this seem improbable? Is it possible that the critic who
flayed allegory as used by Hawthorne because the technique was
too artificial and transparent could himself be guilty of the heresy
of an allegorical and didactic damning of the Negro from the beginning to the end of time? I will not labor the point that Poe, as critic
and fictionist, was no friend of the Negro. This is common knowledge, and as Levin puts it,

> The "constant tendency to the south" in . . . *Pym* takes on a special
> inflection, when we are mindful of the Southern self-consciousness of
> the author. His letters and articles reveal him as an unyielding up-
> holder of slavery, and as no great admirer of the Negro. . . . In the
> troubled depths of Poe's unconscious, there must have been not only
> the fantasy of a lost heritage, but a resentment and a racial phobia.

Jupiter in "The Gold Bug," Toby in "The Journal of Julius Rodman," and others are indeed "comic stereotypes"; and Poe is tickled by Jim Jumble, who, in Bird's *Sheppard Lee,* declines to be set free, by the "old negro wench Juana (all lips)" in Tucker's *George Balcombe,* by the "shovel-footed negro who waddles across the stage" in Ingraham's *Lafitte.* In the simians of such tales as "Rue Morgue," "Marie Roget," "Hop-Frog," and "The System of Dr. Tarr and Professor Fether," there is perhaps a hint, as Levin shows, of "an old Southern bugbear: the fear of exposing a mother or a sister to the suspected brutality of a darker race." When Lowell in his *Fable for Critics* wrote,

> Here comes Poe with his raven, like Barnaby Rudge—
> Three-fifths of him genius, and two-fifths sheer fudge,

it was not so much these lines that inflamed Poe as those which read,

> Forty fathers of freedom, of whom twenty bred
> Their sons for the rice swamps at so much a head,
> And their daughters for—faugh! . . .

Whether berating Lowell as "the Anacharsis Cloots of American letters," the "most rabid of the Abolition fanatics," no book of whose a Southerner would touch, or warning his readers against "giving a second thought to the political philosophies of Madame Trollope" or "the sturdy prejudices" of Fanny Kemble, or praising Thomas Hood's "squib against Abolitionism," Poe, as Killis Campbell long ago pointed out, held blacks, at best, in "good-natured contempt." And sometimes he is less than good-natured. "In his character of Nigger Tom," he writes in his review of *Sheppard Lee,* "[Bird] gives us some very excellent chapters upon abolition and the exciting effects of incendiary pamphlets and pictures, among our slaves in the South. This part of the narrative closes with a spirited picture of a negro insurrection, and with the hanging of Nigger Tom." Although T. O. Mabbott tells us that Poe had a Negro friend, one Armistead Gordon (is Arthur Gordon an echo?), who was "the most interesting man he had ever talked to," it is young Edgar who writes to his foster father: "You suffer me to be subjected to the whims of caprice, not only of your white family, but the complete authority of the blacks."

All this is clear enough. But what Poe was after went deeper than contempt for the Negro. "Great geniuses are parts of the times, they themselves are the times and possess a correspondent coloring," Melville once said. Poe, who has seemed to many an anguished man set apart from his times, was, in fact, a part of the "American Nightmare." In the decade of the founding of Garrison's *Liberator,* of Nat Turner's conspiracy, of the formation of the American Anti-Slavery Society, of Theodore Weld's *The Bible Against Slavery,* he felt called upon to say a more basic piece—to show that slavemasters "violated no law divine or human," to defend the pigmentocracy in his own way. Thus, in reviewing Paulding's *Slavery in the United States*[8] the year before *Pym* came off the press, he enthusiastically seconds its scriptural-genetic defense of slavery, "the basis of all our institutions." The argument, as he sees it, rests on the "peculiar nature" of the Negro.

> Let us reason upon it as we may, there is certainly a power, in causes inscrutable to us, which works essential changes in the different races of animals. . . . The color of the negro no man can deny, and therefore it was but the other day, that they who will believe nothing they cannot account for, made this manifest fact an authority for denying the truth of holy writ. Then comes the opposite extreme—they are, like ourselves, the sons of Adam, and must therefore, have like passions and wants and feelings and tempers in all respects. This, we deny. . . .

"Our theory is a short one," he concludes. *"It was the will of God it should be so."*

Poe was an expert arranger of nature to suit his themes. In "The Domain of Arnheim," the hero sees his fulfillment as poet in the creation of a magnificent landscape:

> A poet, having very unusual pecuniary resources, might, while retaining the necessary idea of art . . . so imbue his designs at once with extent and novelty of beauty, as to convey the sentiment of spiritual interference . . . nature in the sense of the handiwork of the angels that hover between man and God.

Tsalal was no garden of beauty but the intent was the same. It was the "will of God" that Poe tried to present in his allegory of black and white at the end of *Pym.*

---

[8] The review of Paulding was written, in fact, by Judge Nathaniel Beverly Tucker, Professor of Law at William and Mary College. Poe printed it in the *Southern Literary Messenger* for April 1836. On May 2, 1836, he wrote Tucker that he had made "a few immaterial alterations" in it. (William D. Hull, Jr., "A Canon of the Critical Works of Edgar Allan Poe," doctoral dissertation, University of Virginia, 1940, pp. 123-24.)

The Question of Poe's Narrators

by James W. Gargano

Part of the widespread critical condescension toward Edgar Allan Poe's short stories undoubtedly stems from impatience with what is taken to be his "cheap" or embarrassing Gothic style. Finding turgidity, hysteria, and crudely poetic overemphasis in Poe's works, many critics refuse to accept him as a really serious writer. Lowell's flashy indictment of Poe as "two-fifths sheer fudge" [1] agrees essentially with Henry James's magisterial declaration that an "enthusiasm for Poe is the mark of a decidedly primitive stage of reflection." [2] T. S. Eliot seems to be echoing James when he attributes to Poe "the intellect of a highly gifted young person before puberty." [3] Discovering in Poe one of the fountainheads of American obscurantism, Ivor Winters condemns the incoherence, puerility, and histrionics of his style. Moreover, Huxley's charge that Poe's poetry suffers from "vulgarity" of spirit, has colored the views of critics of Poe's prose style.[4]

Certainly, Poe has always had his defenders. One of the most brilliant of modern critics, Allen Tate finds a variety of styles in Poe's works; although Tate makes no high claims for Poe as stylist, he nevertheless points out that Poe could, and often did, write with lucidity and without Gothic mannerisms.[5] Floyd Stovall, a long

"The Question of Poe's Narrators," by James W. Gargano. From *College English*, XXV (December 1963), 177-81. © 1963 by James W. Gargano. Reprinted by permission of the author and The National Council of Teachers of English.

[1] "A Fable for Critics," *The Complete Poetical Works of James Russell Lowell* (Cambridge, 1896), p. 140.

[2] Henry James, "Charles Baudelaire," *French Poets and Novelists* (London, 1878), p. 76.

[3] T. S. Eliot, *From Poe to Valéry* (New York, 1948), p. 28.

[4] Aldous Huxley, "Vulgarity in Literature," *Music at Night and Other Essays* (London, 1949), pp. 297-309.

[5] Allen Tate, "Our Cousin, Mr. Poe," *The Man of Letters in the Modern World*, Meridian Books, pp. 132-145.

time and more enthusiastic admirer of Poe, has recently paid his critical respects to "the conscious art of Edgar Allan Poe." [6] Though he says little about Poe's style, he seems to me to suggest that the elements of Poe's stories, style for example, should be analyzed in terms of Poe's larger artistic intentions. Of course, other writers, notably Edward H. Davidson, have done much to demonstrate that an intelligible rationale informs Poe's best work.[7]

It goes without saying that Poe, like other creative men, is sometimes at the mercy of his own worst qualities. Yet the contention that he is fundamentally a bad or tawdry stylist appears to me to be rather facile and sophistical. It is based, ultimately, on the untenable and often unanalyzed assumption that Poe and his narrators are identical literary twins and that he must be held responsible for all their wild or perfervid utterances; their shrieks and groans are too often conceived as emanating from Poe himself. I believe, on the contrary, that Poe's narrators possess a character and consciousness distinct from those of their creator. These protagonists, I am convinced, speak their own thoughts and are the dupes of their own passions. In short, Poe understands them far better than they can possibly understand themselves. Indeed, he often so designs his tales as to show his narrators' limited comprehension of their own problems and states of mind; the structure of many of Poe's stories clearly reveals an ironical and comprehensive intelligence critically and artistically ordering events so as to establish a vision of life and character which the narrator's very inadequacies help to "prove."

What I am saying is simply that the total organization or completed form of a work of art tells more about the author's sensibility than does the report or confession of one of its characters. Only the most naïve reader, for example, will credit as the "whole truth" what the narrators of *Barry Lyndon, Huckleberry Finn,* and *The Aspern Papers* will divulge about themselves and their experiences. In other words, the "meaning" of a literary work (even when it has no narrator) is to be found in its fully realized form; for only the entire work achieves the resolution of the tensions, heterogeneities, and individual visions which make up the parts. The Ro-

[6] Floyd Stovall, "The Conscious Art of Edgar Allan Poe," *College English,* XXIV (March 1963), 417-421.

[7] Davidson, *Poe: A Critical Study* (Cambridge, 1957).

mantic apologists for Milton's Satan afford a notorious example of the fallacy of interpreting a brilliantly integrated poem from the point of view of its most brilliant character.

The structure of Poe's stories compels realization that they are more than the effusions of their narrators' often disordered mentalities. Through the irony of his characters' self-betrayal and through the development and arrangement of his dramatic actions, Poe suggests to his readers ideas never entertained by the narrators. Poe intends his readers to keep their powers of analysis and judgment ever alert; he does not require or desire complete surrender to the experience of the sensations being felt by his characters. The point of Poe's technique, then, is not to enable us to lose ourselves in strange or outrageous emotions, but to see these emotions and those obsessed by them from a rich and thoughtful perspective. I do not mean to advocate that, while reading Poe, we should cease to feel; but feeling should be "simultaneous" with an analysis carried on with the composure and logic of Poe's great detective, Dupin. For Poe is not merely a Romanticist; he is also a chronicler of the consequences of the Romantic excesses which lead to psychic disorder, pain, and disintegration.

Once Poe's narrative method is understood, the question of Poe's style and serious artistry returns in a new guise. Clearly, there is often an aesthetic compatibility between his narrators' hypertrophic language and their psychic derangement; surely, the narrator in "Ligeia," whose life is consumed in a blind rage against his human limitations, cannot be expected to consider his dilemma in coolly rational prose. The language of men reaching futilely towards the ineffable always runs the risk of appearing more flatulent than inspired. Indeed, in the very breakdown of their visions into lurid and purple rhetoric, Poe's characters enforce the message of failure that permeates their aspirations and actions. The narrator in "Ligeia" blurts out, in attempting to explain his wife's beauty in terms of its "expression": "Ah, words of no meaning!" He rants about "incomprehensible anomalies," "words that are impotent to convey," and his inability to capture the "inexpressible." He raves because he cannot explain. His feverish futility of expression, however, cannot be attributed to Poe, who with an artistic "control," documents the stages of frustration and fantastic desire which end in the narrator's madness. The completed action of "Ligeia," then, comments on the narrator's career of self-delusion and exonerates Poe from the charge of lapsing into self-indulgent, sentimental rodomantade.

In "The Tell-Tale Heart" the cleavage between author and narrator is perfectly apparent. The sharp exclamations, nervous questions, and broken sentences almost too blatantly advertise Poe's conscious intention; the protagonist's painful insistence [on] "proving" himself sane only serves to intensify the idea of his madness. Once again Poe presides with precision of perception at the psychological drama he describes. He makes us understand that the voluble murderer has been tortured by the nightmarish terrors he attributes to his victim: "He was sitting up in bed listening;—just as I have done, night after night, harkening to the death watches in the wall"; further the narrator interprets the old man's groan in terms of his own persistent anguish: "Many a night, just at midnight, when all the world slept, it has welled up from my own bosom, deepening, with its dreadful echo, the terrors that distracted me." Thus, Poe, in allowing his narrator to disburden himself of his tale, skillfully contrives to show also that he lives in a haunted and eerie world of his own demented making.

Poe assuredly knows what the narrator never suspects and what, by the controlled conditions of the tale, he is not meant to suspect— that the narrator is a victim of his own self-torturing obsessions. Poe so manipulates the action that the murder, instead of freeing the narrator, is shown to heighten his agony and intensify his delusions. The watches in the wall become the ominously beating heart of the old man, and the narrator's vaunted self-control explodes into a frenzy that leads to self-betrayal. I find it almost impossible to believe that Poe has no serious artistic motive in "The Tell-Tale Heart," that he merely revels in horror and only inadvertently illuminates the depths of the human soul. I find it equally difficult to accept the view that Poe's style should be assailed because of the ejaculatory and crazy confession of his narrator.

For all of its strident passages, "William Wilson" once again exhibits in its well-defined structure a sense of authorial poise which contrasts markedly with the narrator's confusion and blindness. Wilson's story is organized in six parts: a rather "over-written" *apologia* for his life; a long account of his early student days at Dr. Bransby's grammar school, where he is initiated into evil and encounters the second Wilson; a brief section on his wild behavior at Eton; an episode showing his blackguardly conduct at Oxford; a nondramatic description of his flight from his namesake-pursuer; and a final, climactic scene in which he confronts and kills his "double." The incidents are so arranged as to trace the "development" of Wilson's wickedness and moral blindness. Moreover, Poe's conscious artistic purpose is evident in the effective functioning of many details of symbolism and setting. "Bright rays" from a lamp enable Wilson to see his nemesis "vividly" at Dr. Bransby's; at the critical appearance of his double at Eton, Wilson's perception is obscured by a "faint light"; and in the scene dealing with Wilson's exposé at Oxford, the darkness becomes almost total and the intruder's presence is "felt" rather than seen. Surely, this gradual extinction of light serves to point up the darkening of the narrator's vision. The setting at Dr. Bransby's school, where it was impossible to determine "upon which of its two stories one happened to be," cleverly enforces Poe's theme of the split consciousness plaguing Wilson. So, too, does the portrait of the preacher-pastor:

> This reverend man, with countenance so demurely benign, with robes so glossy and so clerically flowing, with wig so minutely powdered, so rigid and so vast,—could this be he who, of late, with sour visage and in snuffy habiliments, administered, ferule in hand, the Draconian laws of the academy? Oh, gigantic paradox, too utterly monstrous for solution!

Finally, the masquerade setting in the closing scene of the tale ingeniously reveals that Wilson's whole life is a disguise from his own identity.

To maintain that Poe has stumbled into so much organization as can be discovered in "William Wilson" and his other tales requires the support of strong prejudice. There seems little reason for resisting the conclusion that Poe knows what ails Wilson and sees through his narrator's lurid self-characterization as a "victim to the horror and the mystery of the wildest of all sublunary visions." Assuredly, a feeling for the design and subtlety of Poe's "William Wilson" should exorcise the idea that he is as immature and "desperate" as his protagonist. After all, Poe created the situations in which Wilson confronts and is confronted by his *alter ego;* it is Wilson who refuses to meet, welcome, and be restrained by him.

Evidence of Poe's "seriousness" seems to me indisputable in "The

Cask of Amontillado," a tale which W. H. Auden has belittled.[8] Far from being his author's mouthpiece, the narrator, Montresor, is one of the supreme examples in fiction of a deluded rationalist who cannot glimpse the moral implications of his planned folly. Poe's fine ironic sense makes clear that Montresor, the stalker of Fortunato, is both a compulsive and pursued man; for in committing a flawless crime against another human being, he really (like Wilson and the protagonist in "The Tell-Tale Heart") commits the worst of crimes against himself. His reasoned, "cool" intelligence weaves an intricate plot which, while ostensibly satisfying his revenge, despoils him of humanity. His impeccably contrived murder, his weird mask of goodness in an enterprise of evil, and his abandonment of all his life energies in one pet project of hate convict him of a madness which he mistakes for the inspiration of genius. The brilliant masquerade setting of Poe's tale intensifies the theme of Montresor's apparently successful duplicity; Montresor's ironic appreciation of his own deviousness seems further to justify his arrogance of intellect. But the greatest irony of all, to which Montresor is never sensitive, is that the "injuries" supposedly perpetrated by Fortunato are illusory and that the vengeance meant for the victim recoils upon Montresor himself. In immolating Fortunato, the narrator unconsciously calls him the "noble" Fortunato and confesses that his own "heart grew sick." Though Montresor attributes this sickness to "the dampness of the catacombs," it is clear that his crime has begun to "possess" him. We see that, after fifty years, it remains the obsession of his life; the meaning of his existence resides in the tomb in which he has, symbolically, buried himself. In other words, Poe leaves little doubt that the narrator has violated his own mind and humanity, that the external act has had its destructive inner consequences.

The same artistic integrity and seriousness of purpose evident in "The Cask of Amontillado" can be discovered in "The Black Cat." No matter what covert meanings one may find in this much-discussed story, it can hardly be denied that the nameless narrator does not speak for Poe. Whereas the narrator, at the beginning of his "confession," admits that he cannot explain the events which overwhelmed him, Poe's organization of his episodes provides an un-

---

[8] Auden, "Introduction" to *Edgar Allan Poe: Selected Prose and Poetry,* Rinehart Editions, p. v.

mistakable clue to his protagonist's psychic deterioration. The tale
has two distinct, almost parallel parts: in the first, the narrator's inner moral collapse is presented in largely symbolic narrative; in the
second part, the consequence of his self-violation precipitate an
act of murder, punishable by society. Each section of the story deals
with an ominous cat, an atrocity, and an exposé of a "crime." In
the first section, the narrator's house is consumed by fire after he has
mutilated and subsequently hanged Pluto, his pet cat. Blindly, he
refuses to grant any connection between his violence and the fire;
yet the image of a hanged cat on the one remaining wall indicates
that he will be haunted and hag-ridden by his deed. The sinister
figure of Pluto, seen by a crowd of neighbors, is symbolically both
an accusation and a portent, an enigma to the spectators but an
infallible sign to the reader.

In the second section of "The Black Cat," the reincarnated cat
goads the narrator into the murder of his wife. As in "William Wilson," "The Tell-Tale Heart," and "The Cask of Amontillado," the
narrator cannot understand that his assault upon another person
derives from his own moral sickness and unbalance. Like his con-
freres, too, he seeks psychic release and freedom in a crime which
completes his torture. To the end of his life, he is incapable of locat-
ing the origin of his evil and damnation within himself.

The theme of "The Black Cat" is complicated for many critics
by the narrator's dogged assertion that he was pushed into evil and
self-betrayal by the "imp of the perverse." This imp is explained,
by a man who, it must be remembered, eschews explanation, as a
radical, motiveless, and irresistible impulse within the human soul.
Consequently, if his self-analysis is accepted, his responsibility for
his evil life vanishes. Yet, it must be asked if it is necessary to give
credence to the words of the narrator. William Wilson, too, regarded
himself as a "victim" of a force outside himself and Montresor
speaks as if he has been coerced into his crime by Fortunato. The
narrator in "The Black Cat" differs from Wilson in bringing to his
defense a well-reasoned theory with perhaps a strong appeal to many
readers. Still, the narrator's pat explanation is contradicted by the
development of the tale, for instead of being pushed into crime, he
pursues a life which makes crime inevitable. He cherishes the in-
temperate self-indulgence which blunts his powers of self-analysis;
he is guided by his delusions to the climax of damnation. Clearly,

Poe does not espouse his protagonist's theory any more than he approves of the specious rationalizations of his other narrators. Just as the narrator's well-constructed house has a fatal flaw, so the theory of perverseness is flawed because it really explains nothing. Moreover, even the most cursory reader must be struck by the fact that the narrator is most "possessed and maddened" when he most proudly boasts of his self-control. If the narrator obviously cannot be believed at the end of the tale, what argument is there for assuming that he must be telling the truth when he earlier tries to evade responsibility for his "sin" by slippery rationalizations?

A close analysis of "The Black Cat" must certainly exonerate Poe of the charge of merely sensational writing. The final frenzy of the narrator, with its accumulation of superlatives, cannot be ridiculed as an example of Poe's style. The breakdown of the shrieking criminal does not reflect a similar breakdown in the author. Poe, I maintain, is a serious artist who explores the neuroses of his characters with probing intelligence. He permits his narrator to revel and flounder into torment, but he sees beyond the torment to its causes.

In conclusion, then, the five tales I have commented on display Poe's deliberate craftsmanship and penetrating sense of irony. If my thesis is correct, Poe's narrators should not be construed as his mouthpieces; instead they should be regarded as expressing, in "charged" language indicative of their internal disturbances, their own peculiarly nightmarish visions. Poe, I contend, is conscious of the abnormalities of his narrators and does not condone the intellectual ruses through which they strive, only too earnestly, to justify themselves. In short, though his narrators are often febrile or demented, Poe is conspicuously "sane." They may be "decidedly primitive" or "wildly incoherent," but Poe, in his stories at least, is mature and lucid.

The Conscious Art of Edgar Allan Poe

by Floyd Stovall

Although Poe was not the social outcast that Baudelaire conceived him to be, he was, and still is, perhaps the most thoroughly misunderstood of all American writers. His first biographer spread falsehoods about his life and character that a century of truth-telling has failed to dispel. Hence a distorted image of the man has become legendary and perhaps ineradicable in the popular mind. Like other interpreters of Poe, I have learned to live with this distorted image and almost ceased to agonize over it.

Of more immediate concern is the growth during recent decades of an equally distorted image of Poe the artist. I have no quarrel with those who dislike Poe's work so long as they understand it. Woodberry did not like it, yet wrote a fair account of it and of its author; W. C. Brownell did not like it, but he included Poe among the six masters of prose writing in America. I am persuaded that much of the criticism of Poe in this century, whether favorable or unfavorable, has been done by people who have not taken the trouble to understand his work.

Most of Poe's critics fall into one of six categories.

1. Those who simply like to read Poe's poems, tales, and essays. If it is true, as Mr. Eliot says,[1] that Poe had "the intellect of a highly gifted young person before puberty," perhaps these readers, including myself, have intellects similarly retarded. However, persons of some literary reputation have confessed to a liking for Poe's work. In America, Paul Elmer More said, "In three of his essays he has developed his critical theory elaborately and consistently, in *The*

"The Conscious Art of Edgar Allan Poe," by Floyd Stovall. From *College English*, XXIV (March 1963), 417-21. © 1963 by Floyd Stovall. Reprinted by permission of the author and The National Council of Teachers of English.

[1] *From Poe to Valéry* (New York, 1948), p. 19.

Poetic Principle, The Rationale of Verse, and *The Philosophy of Composition,* which together form one of the few aesthetic treatises in English of real value";[2] and, in England, Edith Sitwell says that Poe, "now derided by stupid persons," is the only American poet before Whitman whose work was not "bad and imitative of English poetry." [3]

2. Those who are content to analyze and interpret individual works without evaluating Poe's worth as a writer. These are mostly the academic critics, old-style, to whose work the nonacademic critics, so-called, pay little attention.

3. Those who dislike Poe's writings so thoroughly that they simply cannot see what other intelligent readers appear to see plainly. I have already mentioned Brownell, who nevertheless did praise Poe's prose style. But the critic who qualifies most perfectly in this category is Yvor Winters, who became alarmed more than twenty years ago when, according to his own report, he awakened to the fact that some of his fellow professors had almost established Poe as a great writer while he slept! [4] Mr. Winters finds many errors in Poe's theory, the most flagrant being his alleged failure to distinguish "between matter (truth) and manner (beauty)" and his alleged belief that truth should "be eliminated from poetry, in the interests of a purer poetry." [5]

4. Those who use psychoanalysis as a technique of criticism. D. H. Lawrence's essay in *Studies in Classic American Literature* (1923) was the first influential criticism of this kind. It was soon followed by Joseph Wood Krutch's *Edgar Allan Poe: A Study in Genius* (1926), and by Marie Bonaparte's *Life and Works of Edgar Allan Poe: A Psycho-Analytic Interpretation,* the original French version of which was published in 1933, the English translation in 1949. Other studies, long and short, French and American, have used psychoanalysis to some extent in the search for Poe's hidden secrets. These are not literary critiques at all, but clinical studies of a supposed psychopathic personality. I agree with Allen Tate's apt comment on the psychoanalytic critics in general: "To these ingenious

---

[2] *The Demon of the Absolute* (Princeton, 1928), p. 79.
[3] Preface to *The American Genius* (London, 1951), p. xiii.
[4] *In Defense of Reason* (New York, 1947), p. 234.
[5] *Ibid.,* pp. 240-41.

persons," says Tate, "Poe's works have almost no intrinsic meaning; taken together they make up a *dossier* for the analyst to peruse before Mr. Poe steps into his office for an analysis." [6]

5. Those who like Poe but feel they should not. Perhaps the most notable critic in this category is Mr. Tate himself, who thinks of Poe as a "dejected cousin," [7] and "the transitional figure in modern literature because he discovered our great subject, the disintegration of personality." [8]

6. Those who do not like Poe but feel as if they ought to because certain French writers and critics whom they admire have praised him. T. S. Eliot stands authoritatively at the head of these critics. Though Mr. Eliot calls Poe's intellect "immature" and Paul Valéry's "mature," he traces to Poe two notions which he says were brought to culmination by Valéry: (1) that a poem should have nothing in view but itself, and (2) that the composition of a poem should be as conscious and deliberate as possible.[9]

There are, of course, other ways of looking at Poe's work including my own, for which I claim no originality; indeed, I hope that it is the way of many intelligent readers who have no critical ax to grind. Although a large part of Poe's writing—perhaps more than the two-fifths that Lowell called fudge—is trivial, artistically crude, and often in bad taste, the rest is of literary importance and merits detailed study without reference to its possible autobiographical significance. Some of his poems and tales are difficult, but they can be understood without the help of twentieth century psychology or any greater learning than what can be found in the literature and the reference works to which he had access. I believe the critic should look within the poem or tale for its meaning, and that he should not, in any case, suspect the betrayal of the author's unconscious self until he has understood all that his conscious self has contributed. To affirm that a work of imagination is only a report of the unconscious is to degrade the creative artist to the level of an amanuensis.

I am convinced that all of Poe's poems were composed with conscious art. How else can we account for his frequent and meticulous

[6] "The Angelic Imagination: Poe as God," *Collected Essays* (Denver, 1959), p. 435.

[7] "Our Cousin, Mr. Poe," *op. cit.*, p. 458.

[8] "The Angelic Imagination: Poe as God," *op. cit.*, p. 439.

[9] *From Poe to Valéry*, p. 28.

revision? Most if not all of them had their origin in thought and express or suggest clearly-formed ideas. "Al Aaraaf" was written with the conscious purpose of suggesting Poe's aesthetic theory: that beauty is the province of art, that the artist reveals truth through beauty, and that he must keep his art free of passion. "To Helen" tells how an artist who has been lost on the turbulent seas of passion is restored to his artistic home through the beauty of woman. "Israfel" reminds us that in this imperfect world the poet can approach truth only through the veil of beautiful forms. "The Sleeper" and "The City in the Sea" present a series of images all developed from the trivial idea, or superstition, that those who die rest comfortably in their graves only so long as their surviving friends remember them and mourn. "Dream-Land" is just what the title promises: a description of the topsy-turvy world of dreams. "The Raven" describes the inconsolable grief of a bereaved lover unable to believe in life after death.

Poe did not tell us how he wrote "The Sleeper" and "The City in the Sea," but the several surviving versions of the poems record pretty fully the process of their development. In the earliest version of "The Sleeper" the initial idea was clearly stated, but the passage in which it appeared was later deleted, and so the idea remains only in the images that grew out of it. Certainly all the details were not preformed in his mind before he composed the first draft, but the overall pattern of the poem might well have been. I think it quite possible that "The Raven" was planned in advance of composition very much as Poe says it was in "The Philosophy of Composition." The difference between the early and late poems is chiefly in the technique of composition. The former are predominantly the lyric expression of moods in the style of the English romantic poets, particularly Coleridge; the latter are more dramatic in form, and characterized in style by novelties of rhyme, repetition, metre, and stanza structure, with elements of the fantastic not common before 1840. These novelties of style give the later poems the effect of seeming contrived; and indeed they may have been more completely the work of the deliberate craftsman than the earlier ones.

Analysis of the tales will yield similar results. "Ligeia" relates how the narrator, a student of German transcendentalism, becomes obsessed with the idea that he can, by the power of the will, incorporate his ideal of beauty in the person of a real woman. His first step is to convince himself that such a woman was once his wife; his second step is to impute to her a conscious spirit and the will to live by possessing the body of Rowena, a real woman, whom he has married. Actually the narrator kills Rowena, but attributes her death to the struggle with Ligeia's spirit. Of course the entire action is the hallucination of insanity. Presumably the narrator has recovered some degree of sanity when the story is written down. "The Fall of the House of Usher" describes how discrete objects, by long and close association, may develop a common identity. (Wordsworth suggests the same idea in the story of Margaret in Book I of *The Excursion*.) Roderick Usher is so sure of his identity with his twin sister that he will not believe that she can be dead while he himself still lives. The story ends with the strange invented episode of Ethelred and the dragon, which induces in both Roderick and the narrator (who has been affected also by his friend's theory of identity) the hallucination of Madeline's escape from the tomb and appearance before them. The destruction of the house by storm at the time of Roderick's death seems to validate the theory. "William Wilson" is the story of a wilful and imaginative boy who becomes obsessed with the idea that a schoolmate by the same name, whose good conduct is a reproof to his own selfish egotism, is an embodiment of his own conscience. Wilson leaves school and never sees the other boy again, but the obsession grows upon him so that at intervals afterward he imagines his namesake intervenes to prevent some dishonorable action. Eventually William Wilson imagines he kills his personified conscience and thereafter acts without restraint. He too is apparently insane but recovers sufficiently to write the story of his life.

The origin of these and other imaginative tales was intellectual, but they differ from the tales of ratiocination in presenting their ideas less directly and in achieving their final effect through action rather than through logical analysis. Dupin solves the mystery of "The Murders in the Rue Morgue" because he brings the poetic imagination to the aid of the mathematician's logical reasoning. In "The Purloined Letter" Poe's hero almost meets his match in the Minister D—who is, like Dupin, a poet as well as a mathematician.

Poe's criticism is less difficult than his tales and poems. His theory of the short story is stated, in essence, in the well-known paragraph of his review of Hawthorne's *Twice-Told Tales,* where he says the writer first deliberately conceives the single effect to be wrought, and then invents such incidents, arranges them in such order, and presents them in such a tone as will produce on the reader the preconceived effect. He adds that for fullest satisfaction, the story must be read with an art akin to that of its creator.

Poe's theory of poetry is similar, though less simply stated. According to this theory, every person is endowed by nature with the Poetic Sentiment, or Sentiment of Beauty, an insatiable desire to experience that Supernal Beauty which Poe conceived in Platonic terms as beyond the power of finite man wholly to possess. In this sense, Beauty is an effect, not an attribute. Sensuous beauty, the beauty of natural objects and artistic creations, though it is not an effect but only an attribute, is yet capable of evoking the Sentiment of Beauty, which is an effect, and thus furthering the soul's progress toward Supernal Beauty. Those who have found fault with Poe's definition of Beauty as an effect, not a quality, have failed to weigh sufficiently the sentence in "The Poetic Principle" in which Poe describes man's sense of the beautiful in language reminiscent of Plato as the "struggle, by multiform combinations among the things and thoughts of Time, to attain a portion of that Loveliness whose very elements, perhaps, appertain to eternity alone."

Though Poe denies the poet the use of the didactic method of inculcating the truths of the intellect and the moral sense, he insists that the true poet can and must suggest Truth through Beauty. He believes, with Emerson, that the Good, the True, and the Beautiful are aspects of one divine Unity; that though they are approached by different means, they are identical under the aspect of eternity. As he says in "Eureka," a work of art is necessarily true, and an intellectual structure, because of the harmony of its elements, is necessarily beautiful. Indeed, as stated above, the imaginative and analytic faculties work best when they work together. The scientist uses intuitive reasoning, and the poet requires constructive skill. In "Eureka" he calls Kepler a greater man than Newton because Kepler imagined, or "guessed," the physical laws which Newton later demonstrated rationally to be true. This is not to say that Newton had no imagination, but only that Kepler had more.

If modern skeptics would read "Eureka" carefully and without prejudice, as Paul Valéry did, they might not be so ready to scoff at Poe's account of writing "The Raven" in "The Philosophy of

Composition." Poe means that the poem began in the Poetic Sentiment, was shaped by the imagination, and then constructed according to the imagined pattern with deliberate and methodical skill in the manner best calculated to evoke in the reader the mood from which it grew in the mind of the poet. In short, "The Raven," and with certain necessary individual differences, every other poem Poe wrote, was the product of conscious effort by a healthy and alert intelligence.

Chronology of Important Dates

1809	Edgar Poe born, Boston, January 19, son of Elizabeth Arnold Poe, a talented English actress, and David Poe, a less talented American actor.
1810	Apparently deserted by David, Elizabeth Poe takes her three children to Richmond.
1811	Elizabeth Poe dies, December 18. John Allan, a tobacco exporter, and his wife take Edgar Poe into their home but do not legally adopt him. Renamed Edgar Allan Poe.
1815-20	Accompanies Allans to Great Britain, attending the Manor House School at Stoke Newington, near London, and other schools.
1820-25	Returns to Richmond. Befriended by Mrs. Jane Stith Stanard ("Helen"), who dies in 1824. Begins to write poetry.
1826	Student at University of Virginia (February-December). Academic record good but gambling runs him into debt. Because Allan refuses to pay his debts, Poe cannot return to the University. Sarah Elmira Royster, his sweetheart, becomes engaged to another man.
1827	Quarrels with Allan over debts. *Tamerlane and Other Poems.* Enlists in U. S. Army under alias Edgar A. Perry.
1829	After death of Mrs. Allan, becomes reconciled with Allan. Sergeant-Major "Perry" secures honorable discharge from Army. *Al Aaraaf, Tamerlane, and Minor Poems.*
1830	Enters West Point.
1831	Despairing of securing financial aid from Allan, he decides that a career in the Army is impossible. Disobeys orders and is dismissed from West Point. *Poems.* Takes up residence in the Baltimore home of his aunt Mrs. Maria Clemm.
1832	"Metzengerstein" and four other stories published in the *Philadelphia Saturday Courier.*
1833	"MS Found in a Bottle" wins $50 prize offered by the *Baltimore Saturday Visiter.*
1834	Allan dies, leaving Poe nothing.
1835	Assistant editor of the *Southern Literary Messenger,*

Richmond. Marries his cousin Virginia Clemm (born 1822).

1837   Leaves *Southern Literary Messenger*. Takes Virginia and Mrs. Clemm to New York.

1838   *The Narrative of Arthur Gordon Pym*. Moves with family to Philadelphia.

1839   Literary editor of *Burton's Gentleman's Magazine*. *Tales of the Grotesque and Arabesque*.

1841   Editor of *Graham's Magazine*. Meets Rufus Wilmot Griswold.

1842   Turns to free-lance journalism.

1844   Moves to New York. Becomes "critic and sub-editor" of N. P. Willis's *New York Evening Mirror*.

1845   Leaves the *Mirror* and joins the *Broadway Journal* as one of its three editors, soon becoming sole editor and proprietor. Publishes "The Raven." *Tales. The Raven and Other Poems*.

1846   *Broadway Journal* fails. Moves to a cottage at Fordham, then thirteen miles outside New York City.

1847   Virginia, long in precarious health, dies on January 30.

1848   Poe thinks himself in love with the poetess Sarah Helen Whitman (the Helen of the second "To Helen") and with Mrs. Charles Richmond ("Annie"). Mrs. Whitman first accepts his proposal, then breaks off their engagement. Delivers lectures, including "the Poetic Principle." *Eureka*.

1849   "Annabel Lee." In Richmond for a lecture, he meets Sarah Royster Shelton, his boyhood sweetheart, now a widow, and becomes engaged to her. On October 7 he dies in Baltimore under circumstances which remain mysterious.

Notes on the Editor and Authors

ROBERT REGAN, the editor, is Assistant Professor of English at the University of Virginia. He is the author of *Unpromising Heroes: Mark Twain and His Characters*.

ROY P. BASLER, Director of the Reference Department of the Library of Congress, is the editor of *The Collected Works of Abraham Lincoln*.

MAURICE BEEBE, Professor of English at Purdue University, is the editor of *Modern Fiction Studies* and the author of numerous critical works.

JAMES W. GARGANO, Professor of English at Washington and Jefferson College in Pennsylvania, has published a number of articles on nineteenth century American writers. In 1963-64 he was Fulbright lecturer at the University of Caen.

ALDOUS HUXLEY, one of the most distinguished novelists, satirists, and philosophers of the twentieth century, died in 1963.

SIDNEY KAPLAN, Professor of English at the University of Massachusetts, has edited Melville's *Battle Pieces* and Poe's *Gorden Pym*.

JOSEPH WOOD KRUTCH, critic, biographer, naturalist, and philosopher, retired as Professor of Dramatic Literature at Columbia University in 1950. He has since made his home in Arizona.

PATRICK F. QUINN, Associate Professor of English at Wellesley College, has written extensively on Poe.

JOSEPH PATRICK ROPPOLO, Associate Professor of English at Tulane University, has written on subjects ranging from Chaucer to the modern theater. His most recent publication is *Philip Barry*.

FLOYD STOVALL is Edgar Allan Poe Professor of English at the University of Virginia. He is the author of *American Idealism* and many other studies in criticism and literary history and is editor of *The Poems of Edgar Allan Poe*.

ALLEN TATE, poet, critic, novelist, and teacher, was a leader of the Fugitive Group of Southern agrarians in the 1920s. His poetry has won many awards, including the Bollingen poetry prize. He is now Professor of English at the University of Minnesota.

JEAN-PAUL WEBER, well known in France as critic and philosopher, is the author of *La Psychologie de l'Art* and several other books. In 1965-66 he was visiting Associate Professor at the City University of New York.

RICHARD WILBUR, whose first book of poems, *The Beautiful Changes,* won the Pultizer Prize in 1957, has published translations of Molière's *Misanthrope* and *Tartuffe* and an edition of Poe's poems as well as several volumes of his own verse. He is now Professor of English at Wesleyan University in Connecticut.

Selected Bibliography

"It can still be said that it is the shame of American scholarship that there is no complete and accurate text of all Poe's writings." So the late James Southall Wilson wrote in 1942. The situation today is less shameful only as regards Poe's poetry, which Floyd Stovall has presented in an edition admirable alike for bibliographical scholarship and book design, *The Poems of Edgar Allan Poe* (Charlottesville, 1965). Until the long-awaited edition of the whole of the canon being prepared by T. O. Mabbott appears, the Virginia Edition of *The Complete Works of Edgar Allan Poe,* edited by James A. Harrison (New York, 1902), 17 vols., must remain the standard authority for the text of the prose. Poe's correspondence is available in the excellent edition of John Ward Ostrom, *The Letters of Edgar Allan Poe* (2 vols.; Cambridge, Mass., 1948).

Arthur Hobson Quinn's *Edgar Allan Poe: A Critical Biography* (New York, 1941) gained soon after its appearance universal recognition as the primary authority on questions of Poe's life. Two earlier biographies, however, remain of more than historical interest: Hervey Allen's *Israfel: The Life and Times of Edgar Allan Poe* (New York, 1929; revised 1934) and George E. Woodberry's *The Life of Edgar Allan Poe* (Boston, 1885; revised 1909). The most reliable recent work on Poe's life is Edward Wagenknecht's *Edgar Allan Poe: The Man Behind the Legend* (New York, 1963), a sane and trustworthy presentation of the man and the artist which will appeal to the nonspecialist because of its brevity and informality.

Bibliographical guidance to the extensive critical literature on Poe is available in Jay B. Hubbell's essay in Floyd Stovall, ed., *Eight American Authors: A Review of Research and Criticism* (New York, 1956; 2nd ed. with bibliographical supplement, 1963). Reviews of new books on Poe and a current bibliography of criticism appear regularly in *American Literature.* Several of the essays in this collection, notably those of Messrs. Stovall, Gargano, Quinn, and Roppolo, discuss and evaluate the best-known articles and books on Poe. The shortcomings of recent Poe criticism and scholarship are perceptively discussed in Stuart Levine's article "Scholarly Strategy: The Poe Case," *American Quarterly,* XVII (Spring 1965), 133-44.

TWENTIETH CENTURY VIEWS

American Authors